BEYOND BROKEN Families

Ezekiel's Vision of Hope for Marriages

Kathleen McAnear Smith

DESTINY IMAGE™ EUROPE srl
Via Maiella, 1
66020 San Giovanni Teatino (Ch) – Italy

"Changing the world, one book at a time."™

This book and all other Destiny Image™ Europe books are available at Christian bookstores and distributors worldwide.

To order products, or for any other correspondence:

DESTINY IMAGE™ EUROPE srl
Via della Scafa 29/14
65013 Città Sant'Angelo (Pe), Italy
Tel. +39 085 4716623 • +39 085 8670146
Fax: +39 085 9090113

Email: info@eurodestinyimage.com
Or reach us on the Internet: www.eurodestinyimage.com

ISBN 13: 978-88-96727-33-1
ISBN 13 Ebook: 978-88-96727-41-6

For Worldwide Distribution, Printed in Italy.
1 2 3 4 5 6 7 / 15 14 13 12 11

*This book is dedicated in loving memory
to my mother, Elizabeth Ostwalt McAnear —
she never stopped praying for all of us.*

ACKNOWLEDGMENTS

Above all, I give thanks for the story Jesus Christ, through His Holy Spirit, placed in my spirit to share with you in *Beyond Broken Families*. Without Jesus, there would be no story, and it is my hope that throughout this book you will see all that the Lord has done!

I give thanks for Chris, the husband God gave me on this recovery road, in this third season of life. Chris supported the vision the Lord gave me. I knew God called me to write this story, this testimony to His way of healing, but Chris came and enabled the writing space, the time—and his prayer covered me as I went into battle with words on a laptop.

I give thanks for encouragement to write from Angela and Dave Watkinson, my much loved daughter and son-in-law. They continue to be a blessing and inspiration to the whole family.

I give thanks for my much loved son, Mark Cocklin. He inspired me in this story. His humor as well as technological ability (including breaking down file zipping so even Mom understands is no small feat for a modern-day computer programmer) have been a great support.

I give thanks for friends including Gay Mallam, Joyce and Bill Wright, Marlene Cantor, Kay and Tom Thompson, Janet Chester, Leslie King, Lisa Young, and Jane Mahy who have lived part of this story with me. I give thanks for friends who have listened as I talked and talked and wrote the pages of this testimony, always to keep it grounded in reality of what God is doing, actually doing. Sonya Kyte listened to chapter upon chapter.

I give thanks for Doctors Jim and Joy McInnis, our pastors at Fisherman's Net Revival Center in Venice, Florida, for their teaching, love, and outstanding support as I began this recovery journey. I would fly back to Florida straight from England, totally exhausted from all that was going on at the time; even once putting my head on the table to sleep after an overnight flight to attend the women's meeting. Pastor Joy as well as my dear friends Onida Mello and Delores Balla in the leadership team were and are truly Titus 2 women who knew and know exactly how to strengthen my hands for the joy of family life ahead. Because of this team, I am passionate about women's ministry!

I give thanks for Roz Parker and Neil Dupres, pastors of Frensham Baptist Fellowship, and Lindy Dupres, all from our English church.

I give thanks for all I learned from Holy Trinity Brompton Church in London, especially Eric who led the Divorce and Separation Recovery group, and Rose who lovingly served the meals at each class. The works of your hands were duly established and blessed us all.

I give thanks for all I learned from Ellel Ministries UK. My dear friend Rosalinde Joosten helped give clarity to what I wanted to say in these pages. I especially want to give thanks for Jill Southern Jones at Ellel Pierrepont in Surrey. It was because of Jill standing up one day and reading out loud the whole of Ezekiel 34 that I wrote this book. It would take several books to begin to tell all I have learned from Jill.

I give thanks for my prayer partners, Crusita Sosa (who listened to me read many of the earlier versions) in Florida and Pam Kincaid in England. I pay tribute to Pam, as she "passed away" this year, saying, "I have an appointment with the King."

I give great thanks for the publishing team at Destiny Image Europe. It is such an honor to work with you. Destiny Image Europe's staff, including Angela in the U.S., have the eagle's eye for correction and the Father's gift of encouragement. Pietro Evangelista leads the European team, as Brother Berhanu, Sister Marzia, and Brother Michael follow the Lord's leading to train and equip yet another generation of writers to give glory to the Lord Jesus Christ.

Last but not least, I wish to give thanks for my sister, Dr. Mary Black, and my brother, Tom McAnear. We were there for each other as Mom went for her own appointment with the King. We give thanks for each other, and for that I give thanks.

ENDORSEMENTS

There is at least one time in every person's life when they need to tell their story and know they have been heard. Listening is the gift of God's heart to help us work in cooperation with his Holy Spirit so that we make sure we grow through all those issues that challenge or choke our desire to move on with God. I am happy to endorse *Beyond Broken Families* because it champions the gift of listening and will be a healing experience for all those who read it and take up its challenge.

Rev. Dr. Russ Parker, Director
Acorn Christian Healing Foundation

As a survivor of abuse as a child, including sexual abuse, this book has led me on the path to not only start addressing the issues that I have kept swept under the rug, but to actually start the journey to healing. I shall be an overcomer!

Mrs. K
Church Administrator

I strongly recommend *Beyond Broken Families* as a book that changes lives. As Kathleen recounts her own pilgrimage and personal journey, we see God at work in an extraordinary way. God was able to move powerfully into her life and challenge her old lifestyle, and bring deep-level healing from divorce and pain. This book is the message of the healing power of Jesus Christ for ordinary people and will encourage you to reach out for Him in the same way as Kathleen did.

Jill Southern-Jones
Center Director, Ellel Ministries Pierrepont

Beyond Broken Families is a very practical book to help those going through divorce work through the pain and disappointments in a systematic way with God in order to put derailed families back on track. Kathleen has written deeply personally to show God comforts those who mourn yet at the same time challenges readers to examine their lives with God and face the realities and character developments that are necessary to rebuild their lives.

Rosalinde Joosten
Corporate Leadership, Ellel Ministries UK

CONTENTS

Foreword 11

Preface 13

Chapter 1   The Dream 15

Chapter 2   Holy Trinity Brompton, Monday Night 23

Chapter 3   What it Takes to Be Healed 33

Chapter 4   Let the Sabbatical Begin! 41

Chapter 5   Forgiveness 51

Chapter 6   The Wall of Hostility 67

Chapter 7   The High Pasture 79

Chapter 8   Listening and Boundaries 93

Chapter 9   Why? 105

Chapter 10   Thy Kingdom Come 121

Chapter 11   Frequent Flyer 129

Chapter 12   The Bone Picker 145

Epilogue 163

Endnotes 165

FOREWORD

Family is one of the most awesome gifts God gave to humankind, ever! Because He created family, there is no doubt, as with all of God's creations, it is meant to be successful and for people to enjoy it for a lifetime. Family is designed to satisfy the God-inspired need of fellowship with others. Loneliness is not God's plan for humankind: "The Lord God said, "It is not good for the man to be alone…" (Genesis 2:18).

Marriage is the environment in which family is birthed, gets nurtured, and develops. Love is the ingredient that allows marriage to develop a strong and healthy family in which each member feels accepted, cared for, and valued.

Most Christians believe this about families, I am sure, and countless books have been written on the secrets to have God's dream for us come true. Unfortunately, though, dreams can only come true when people allow God's way to be their way. We have to base all of our decisions and choices on what we know to be God's righteous way—especially when it comes to mending broken families and keeping our families happily together.

Oftentimes, people whose childhoods were lived in an unhealthy family environment where love was not an ingredient perpetuate the same kind of hurtful environment in their families and consequently leave their children with the same, sad inheritance.

In our post-modern society, the number of unhappy marriages and subsequent broken families is increasing outside and inside the church. While many of us keep believing in God's dream for traditional, functionally fit families, we need to provide practical

11

and biblical answers and hope for families that have been torn apart.

This is what *Beyond Broken Families* is all about!

While many Christian authors focus on how to prevent families from breaking apart, Kathleen, in this great book of proven solutions, focuses giving hope to the victims of broken families. If God gave Ezekiel hope for dry bones to rise up and live again, the same hope is true for broken families!

You may be suffering because of strained or broken family relationships or you know people who are—this is the book that will put everything into perspective. There is hope—and help is just a few pages away.

Pietro Evangelista, Publisher,
Destiny Image Europe, Italy

PREFACE

It seems only yesterday I heard the Holy Spirit say to my spirit, "*Just* tell My story," and I knew that word "tell" meant write and speak. Sometimes as these words came to mind, it was "Just" tell my story; and sometimes the emphasis was "just tell *MY* story." Always, the story was meant to be His story in me or through me, for He is our Master Storyteller. His story in all of us is the story worth telling, for the healing of our guarded hearts, for the inspiring of others to share what the Lord has done in their lives.

I was stunned that Father God was as serious as I found Him to be about this recovery stuff. He cared enough about my broken family to *do* something? Yes, He wanted to know I was up for the journey and that I would let Him order my footsteps. But oh what wild treasures He set in place and *is* setting in place as I follow Him. This is no brick road out of Kansas, but the way of finally, truly living in the freedom of His love.

Author's note: As you read this book and I share lessons learned, please know that I am not suggesting that my journey is your journey. If any of what I share is for you, and you want to be healed, restored, forgiven, then I gently challenge you to humbly turn to Jesus, the Shepherd of all shepherds, and commit your journey to Him. Full healing and restoration is a result of making a decision and a commitment to personally journeying with the Shepherd.

…They will live in safety, and no one will make them afraid. Then they will know that I, the Lord their God, am with them and that they, the house of Israel, are My people, declares the Sovereign Lord (Ezekiel 34:28,30).

That which was from the beginning, which we have heard, which we have seen with our eyes, which we have looked at and our hands have touched—this we proclaim concerning the Word of life (1 John 1:1).

Chapter 1

THE DREAM

This book is written for those of you whose dream of whole, holy family life has turned into one long, messed up nightmare. You hardly dare dream of recovering all you have lost, whether it be a marriage, a relationship with your children, or for some of you, even so much as a family meal together. This book is from the heart of Father God through some very broken people including myself, who wish to tell you a story of what the Lord has done and is doing to give hope for people who normally can't keep family life together.

If you despair of ever having an emotionally healthy family, and maybe even now are failing in your marriage, then this book is for you. The glory of this story has to go to God, as I can guarantee the people in this book, no matter how intelligent or full of university degrees or religious motivation, were not capable of coming up with a dream that would work.

I remember flying into New York City one afternoon, getting into the rental car and driving up the freeway. I turned on the radio, and the announcer said, "Well, ladies and gentlemen, I have to announce that for the second year running we have sold out of tickets for the Annual Dysfunctional Family Picnic." For a moment, I just laughed, thinking my family is so dysfunctional we wouldn't even go to the picnic on Jones Beach; but what saddens me is that there are so many families like us!

We—the people in families who do not function in the Bible-nurturing way of the Lord—can be quite capable in our jobs and life outside the home; but once inside the four walls of family life, things seem to fall apart. Many of us turn all the more to work for our emotional need of affirmation, or to drugs or mind games for self-confidence, or to overeating or sex for comfort. We may have won awards and rewards, distinction in all we do in our chosen field, but not in our wildest dreams can we figure out how to have a blessed family life.

This book is for those who believe they have tried everything to have a successful, happy family life and yet all around them they see broken and crushed dreams. They see the dead looks in the eyes of their children and in the checked-out minds of parents and grandparents. We see it in ourselves in very dark nights of despair.

The stories in this book are not to tell you how we have been successful in saving difficult marriages or repaired broken family life, but to share the story of how Father God, in His mercy is giving hope to a new generation. It is His story of a remarkable dream He has given me and others, for recovering family life. In a sense, it is the real "impossible dream," and only as we see it unfold can we begin to dream along with Him who makes all things possible.

The Dream Exchange

Louie, a member of the preaching team at our church, told me about the dream he had while growing up in Germany.

"I had heard Mick Jagger sing," he said, laughing a little, "and I had a dream of being a rock star. I wanted the girls, the drugs, the great life. Then I became a Christian," continued Louie with some bravado, "and so I wanted to be a Christian rock star!"

Louie asked us, in a sermon one Sunday morning, "Do you think Mary, the mother of Jesus, had a dream for her life? She did so well with *God's* dream for her life. And what about Judas? Did he have a dream? And then what about Mohammed? Buddha? Adolf Hitler? Did he have a dream? Did you know that when he finished killing all the Jews, he planned to go on and get rid of the Christians, as he knew we would never truly come under his authority? That was the plan."

"What about those with good dreams? Has Billy Graham fulfilled all his dream?"

Louie asked us to think about the dreams of these people; and just for a moment to ask ourselves how life would be different if those

16

with the destructive dreams had given their dreams to God, for an exchange: Father God's dream for their dream.[1]

"One day," said Louie, "God asked me to go to Bible school. 'Why?' I asked God, 'It's not my dream; and besides, I know everything already.'" We laughed alongside Louie at the personal arrogance of dreams.

"And God said to me, 'Louie, give Me your dream.' Why God? My dream, my idea of being a rock star, never happened. Why do You want my dream?"

"Will you give it to Me?" asked God.

"Sure," said Louie.

"That's good," said God to Louie. "Now I can give you My dream that I have for you."

FATHER GOD'S DREAM FOR FAMILY LIFE

According to Genesis 2:24, marriage as God intended was, "For this reason a man will leave his father and mother and be united to his wife, and they will become one flesh."

Nicky and Sila Lee, in *The Marriage Book*, write that as "Marriage is about two people being joined together to become one…it is therefore the closest most intimate relationship of which human beings are capable."[2]

This was and is God's dream for you and me. His idea for marriage is for us to:

> *Watch what God does, and then you do it, like children who learn proper behavior from their parents. Mostly what God does is love you. Keep company with Him and learn a life of love. Observe how Christ loved us. His love was not cautious but extravagant. He didn't love in order to get something from us but to give everything of Himself to us. Love like that* (Ephesians 5:1-2 TM).

I don't know about you, but I and others in the following chapters did not get the happily-ever-after version of a childhood. It may have seemed like we had the white picket fence, golden girl life, but that certainly wasn't the full story. Even though God had a wonderful plan for our upbringing, I guess some of our parents just didn't read the script. God's plan for a nurturing childhood was intended as training for "How to do Family Life," which would move us on to a true love relationship that would build a family and support a community.

Unfortunately, some of us have no idea what true love looks like. We've never experienced it in our childhood homes, and now we have little idea as to how to establish it in our own homes. Somewhere in the back of our minds we know that love has to be more than a Valentine card. But what is it?

While "modern media has on the whole reduced love to some sentimental, romantic feeling, where people fall in and out of love at the drop of a hat, biblical love is different," says Roz Parker, one of the pastors at Frensham Baptist in Surrey, England.[3] "The Greek word for this love is *agape*, which is the active love of God for His Son and His people. It's not just a sit back and feel good kind of love."[4] A love that never fails is *agape* love. *Agape* is love unconditional, extravagant grace.

The extravagance we see today is more often featured in the weddings of our puffed up dreams or in lifestyles we strive to maintain. We buy the "image" of love. There is many a modern bride who is a demanding "bridezilla"—with only visions of the perfect cake, flowers, and honeymoon dancing around in her head.

Christian brides and grooms dream a bigger dream of family—nurture and support. They dream of a love that is lasting and faithful, encouraging each family member to live life to the full. Even still, we must have a bigger dream.

We want more. We were made to need more.

God has a bigger dream.

God's dream for us is that we love one another as He loves us. As Christ loves the church, so is a man to love his wife. As we build strong marriages, this love spills out to the neighborhood to build strong communities. We are instructed to "love our neighbors as ourselves."

It is a love that is to go out into all the world and make a people who want to learn how to do this love.

But what is this love we are to be blessed with? What blessings are in store for us in God's dream? Love is defined in First Corinthians 13, and Philippians 2:3-4 says, "Do nothing out of selfish ambition or vain conceit, but in humility consider others better than yourselves. Each of you should look not only to your own interests, but also to the interests of others."

God's dream for our family life is read out in so many marriage ceremonies; yet the wedding rings are hardly exchanged before we exchange His dream for our dream. Even as Christians, we want to change each other, changing our spouse to fit our dreams and ambitions. We easily get lost in arguments of love confronts versus love accepts, and believe the lie of the world of credit cards—that we can do anything and have anything, never waiting for anything. At times, we have no idea that our dreams are pushing out Father God's dream for our lives, our marriage, and our families. Often our good dreams push out His best dream.

Father God has many plans for nurturing our family life. He wants so much for us—packing down into our spirits, souls, and bodies blessing upon blessing. Each blessing received is to be a blessing shared, nurturing and challenging us to unite our hearts and minds as one with Him.

When His ways turn out to not be our ways, it seems the stress and striving to reach dreams of our own imagination cause us to lose our way. Temptation comes in so many forms. When we have no idea the origin and source of love, fresh love, we dry up and declare ourselves "at a loss as to what to do."

Sila and Nicky Lee remind us that "marriage thrives on creativity," but that as "we live in a consumerist age in which people are not used to mending things…if it doesn't work it is easier and cheaper to buy a new one."[5] It is indeed so much easier, especially when we have never seen the process of mending or a dry hope come to life.

When we think of people who have married three, four, or more times, as celebrity types are known to do, it seems they have no understanding as to why every time they get on a marriage train, the train breaks down, and then there is a train wreck. Maybe you have been on that train-wreck-waiting-to-happen more than once. Please understand that there is indeed, a wrecker, a destructive enemy who is out to find the weak spots in all our relationships, in every area of our lives, and even life itself. John 10:10 says the enemy has a job description—to "steal and kill and destroy."

But God

Even at the point of multiple family failings, it is time to acknowledge that Father God might (and does) have a dream for you. The second part of John 10:10 is, "I [Jesus] have come that they [you and I] may have life, and have it to the full." God has a plan, and it is for good, not evil, for your life and your family.

I believe that the two best words in the Bible are "but God!" Even though satan may do all he can to steal God's dream of a healthy family life, and he may indeed snatch away our dream—*but God* will not allow him to touch the dream He has for us if we will take hold of it.

It is my hope that, step by step, you will take hold of the dream the Father God Almighty has for you. For those of us who have had little reason to hope, it is no small thing to learn to trust; and yet, when no person we know can be trusted, God can be trusted to teach us to trust Him. *He can help us learn that His plans are for good and not for evil.*

Psalm 25:9 tells us that, "He guides the humble in what is right and teaches them His way." It takes humility to accept the truth that God has a better dream. It takes humility to exchange our dream for His.

The Dream He Gave Me

When I realized that no matter what I did to save my personal dream of family life and it was not working as expected, I more carefully sang the words to the song, "I Surrender All." Now it is "all to Jesus, I surrender." The challenge we face, those of us with broken dreams and broken homes, is that God has a plan for our recovery into an alignment with His plan for our lives.

No matter how off track we are, we can come to the cross where Jesus died for our sins and have the divine exchange of dreams. It may be a long time before God leads you to trust another human this side of Heaven, but you can trust *Him*. As the stories ahead unfold, you will see that He knew from the beginning you were going to mess up in your marriage, your family life; and from the beginning of time, He has had a recovery plan.

I pray that this book will help you get hold of His plan, His dream for your life.

As a shepherd looks after his scattered flock when he is with them, so will I look after My sheep, I will rescue them from all the places where they were scattered on a day of clouds and darkness (Ezekiel 34:12).

Chapter 2

HOLY TRINITY BROMPTON, MONDAY NIGHT

Rose stood behind the table and dished out a lovely dinner. Only on the last night of the Divorce and Separation Recovery class could I look at her. To me, there was so much shame in my family falling part that it was all I could do to travel to London from Winchester and sit with my small group to hear the evening's talk. It took weeks to start entering into the discussions.

Each week there was a new topic such as dealing with the legal system, making good decisions for your children, and the difficult topic of forgiveness. Each week I heard the stories of others in my small group as they dealt with child custody issues or crushing remarks from former spouses or in-laws, or simply dealt with the loneliness of setting up a new "home" that wasn't a home of their own. Many in the class, like me, were Christians and were shocked and exhausted. This wasn't supposed to happen to us.

My personal recovery plan from any pain in my life usually consisted of running away to a safe place—and a little "retail therapy." Dealing with the unbearable, heartbreaking pain of divorce would be no different except that running away and spending money to assuage the pain would be on a damagingly larger scale.

I have a tendency to see no other choice than leave the place of conflict until people can be reasonable, stop hitting, shouting (fill in your own idea of what makes a place not safe). While the Divorce Recovery class was in itself a safe haven, as an American living all her adult life in the United Kingdom, I suddenly felt I could not cope or make any decisions unless I was back on United States soil.

I convinced myself that I needed to leave England and try to think clearly according to my birth culture. So keeping with my pattern of "when the going gets tough, flee the kitchen," it will not surprise you that even after years of living in England and raising my children, I thought nothing of maxing my credit card and getting on a plane to New York, and renting a car to drive to Connecticut to stay a few days with my closest American friend, Marlene Cantor.

Marlene, after twenty-something years of trying to make a marriage work, was also in the middle of divorce. We talked and walked the hilly path around the leafy Connecticut lake where she lived, and we wondered together why so many, many marriages fail. Why couldn't we make things work? Why could we figure out how to have success in other areas of our lives, but not with our spouses?

Marlene is Jewish and I am a Christian; and while both of us would turn to God for the comfort and guidance, we longed for answers to questions such as, "How should we love our husbands? How can we build a strong family life?" We wanted some "how to" answers, if only to pass on to our children.

There are plenty of books on how to have a happy marriage, and over the years my friend and I can honestly tell you we have tried most of the suggestions. I can testify that all we gave and all we did to raise our children in a healthy, happy home with our husbands wasn't enough. The breakdown of our families wasn't from lack of trying. Like many who are experiencing the breakdown of family life, even if there is no divorce or legal separation, we needed recovery from the damage done to our spirits, souls, and bodies. Even if we gained no hope for ourselves, for our children we needed answers so that this damage would not be our only legacy.

DECK TIME

Instead of staying in the room vacated by her daughter who was away at college, I chose to sleep on the oversized couch next to the wall-to-wall glass doors leading to the deck overlooking the lake. Though I would not at the time have recognized that my Personal Recovery Plan (PRP) included being surrounded by natural beauty, it was peace personified to stand out on that deck in the early morning, coffee in hand and watch the Canadian geese slide to a screeching halt on the water. Steam would rise from the surface of the lake, and I could just make out a canoe or two leaving the embankment for sunrise fishing. It was a natural part of my personal recovery to spend a little quiet time on the deck.

During some early morning deck time, God began taking me in hand in a new and quite remarkable way. *How could the sky be this blue this early in the morning?* I wondered. Not a cloud; there was nothing past the trees and over the lake, but totally clear blue sky. I was praying and thanking God for the scene before me, this quiet place, when suddenly a very round ball, looking like a very large ball of wool, floated across the sky. If a skywriter made this formation, I missed seeing any plane. I became quite excited as it reminded me of what my friend, Gay, back in England, had told me about God sorting out my life.

"Your life is a total mess," Gay had said in a way that only close English friends can say. No argument from me. She didn't stop there, "*You* can't sort this out. Only God can sort out your life and make some sort of sense out of it." She told me of how years ago children in England learned to knit at their mother's knee and that when the children couldn't sort out the wool, or they had made a mess of whatever it was they were trying to knit, they would give it to their mother to unravel or unknot and form into a new skein or ball of wool so that something could be "made afresh."

Gay told me to "toss the mess" I had made of my marriage and family life onto my Father God's lap. My life was like a much messed up knotted piece of wool that was unravelling. "Leave it," Gay said, "toss it, cast it on His lap for Him to sort it all out, unknot the knots, and make a new ball of wool for you to begin again. Give it to Him."

Now, with my own eyes, I was seeing a ball of wool in the sky, with one thread hanging down as if ready for me to take hold and to begin to knit again. Quite surprised that this was happening in the clear sky above, I longed for a camera. *No one will believe me,* I thought. As I watched the ball of what looked like wool slowly float across the sky, it dawned on me to go and wake up Marlene.

Knowing that my friend was not a morning person, I quietly went to her room and tried to gently wake her. "Marlene," I said, "I'm so sorry to wake you at this hour, but I have to show you something or no one…not even me…will believe I have seen this in the sky."

With one eye open and in a slight daze, my friend got up and followed me to the deck area. She looked at the sky. With both eyes opened wide, she said "You're right. No one would believe you. That is a ball of wool in the sky. Oh my!"

I told her about Gay saying that I needed to hand my life over to God, as a child who is learning to knit and messes up hands over the wool to be untangled and made ready to knit again. "OK," she said, "so now you know. And you are right. If I hadn't seen this, I never would have believed you." With that said, Marlene went back to bed.

I stayed on the deck until the "wool" rolled out of sight. For the first time, I began to have a little hope. God was sorting out my mess. For one fleeting moment I was curious more than fearful. *How on earth would we—Father God and me—begin to make something of my life and bring back my family?* I wondered.

The Reality Problem

The difficulty with families falling part is that we just don't know what to do with the pain. We want it to go away. We are desperate for things to be different. Some of us want our spouses back, but in a new marriage. As Christians, some of us are on our knees for marriage restoration. Others just want the pain to go away, their difficult spouse to be on another planet, and their new life to begin right away. Oh and we all want our children to not even look or feel as if they have been through the fire that burned their world to the ground.

It is a very great temptation to just shut down the pain. Some religions and some philosophies of positive thinking urge you to rise above the pain. New Age thinking often suggests a mantra, focusing on a word or phrase to get you through the day. Another type of thinking encourages you to "just forget about it," and move on. On to another relationship where, unfortunately, you are bound to divorce again.[1]

How do we get to that place—in our mind, our will, our emotions—where we accept and deal effectively with the reality of a relationship breakdown?

THE LIE

My reality was too much to bear. I bought the lie that I needed to handle life myself; and thus, deal with any pain I had from divorcing my husband after twenty-seven years. I bought the lie that being a responsible person meant I kept the pain under control. That seemed to be the message from the people around me at the time. They did not know what to do with a person in such pain; and frankly, they didn't want to know. They had very busy lives, and a few challenges of their own. What church would be crazy enough to take on the growing social burden of broken families? Church life was busy enough without adding one more program or project.

I bought into the lie that they must be right—who had time for people with this kind of emotional pain? Surely, sinners got what they deserved. It was almost too embarrassing to discuss. Denial of pain seemed the only option. Pain was to be pushed down, or at least not revealed in public. I bought the lie that all I needed to do was "get a grip!"

I took long, hot baths. I did all I needed to do to get through the day. I cried all night.

CHURCH ROLE?

The church I attended at the time of my divorce was brilliant at assisting with practical needs, and for this I give thanks; but they had no idea how to handle the road to recovery for me or my family. I had to travel to London to find the help that I needed—help that would enable me to be the parent I wanted to be, help that would give me a reason to keep on living. The pastor in our small town (at that time) thought that offering Divorce Recovery would only encourage divorce. The result of that decision left many in our church wounded and scattered, bewildered as to where to find help.

It is a great dilemma when we say we want our pastors to understand our suffering in this modern age;[2] and yet at the same time, we want them to live up to the biblical job description. On one hand, we want pastors who are married, with one spouse, faithful to their family and a champion in godly living; yet some wish they were also recovered drug addicts able to understand addiction, divorced able to understand a family break-up, ex-gang members to know street life. We want them to have touched every stove to know the heat of the challenges we face. Often in a time of family crisis, our emotions and need for assistance are not realistic; in this case, it is not even biblical.

God asks, instead, that pastors love the people, having skill and compassion enough to bind up wounds in the flock. God asks that pastors have an agape love,[3] in carrying out the will of the Father for His flock. Though we will talk more about this type of love in later chapters, for now we need to recognize that agape is not for the faint-hearted. It is the challenge of the shepherds.

Being from a family filled with missionaries and pastors as well as doctors and lawyers committed to God's work, I have also seen what happens when a pastor and the leadership team give everything they have, and exhaustingly concede defeat in reaching a much loved, but much emotionally damaged member of their flock. Sometimes this is due to lack of shepherd training, but certainly not a lack of compassion.

Sometimes a sheep is determined, no matter what is done on his or her behalf, to stray and not be found. If you are a church leader, it is my hope that this book will give you deeper understanding of some of the challenges facing lost sheep and encouragement as you take up the challenge of shepherding in a broken world. I give thanks for shepherds with a heart for the lost.

WHAT IS A SHEPHERD?

First of all, a shepherd is not a cowboy. A cowboy goes out and rounds up the herd and drives them on to where he needs them to go. A strong cowboy sends that lasso and drags you in. A shepherd, on the other hand, calmly cares for his or her sheep. He goes after any that are lost—to care for them, and gently carry them home. Those who have watched shepherds in Israel will tell you the sheep know the shepherd's voice and they follow that shepherd; the shepherd does not drive the sheep. He or she watches the flock closely and especially tends to the little ones during lambing season. It is a full-on, full-time job.

In the Bible, Father God tells Ezekiel that leaders, those men and women entrusted with doing God's will on earth in caring for His people, leading them along a path that is meant for them in coming closer to God, knowing His still, small voice, must be a shepherd. His leaders are shepherds, and His son is *The Shepherd*.[4]

Jesus would use choice words, such as "You den of vipers!" to describe those who set up rules and more rules—religion instead of the freedom found in Christ—and yet called themselves, "Rabbi." Jesus made it clear that "God so loved the world that He gave His only son," and that "we would know His sheep by their love." His sheep would know His voice and follow Him. His would be the way, the truth, and life. Jesus would say it is a serious matter and a responsibility to love your flock unconditionally, being a shepherd.

CHALLENGE OF EZEKIEL

This book is subtitled *Ezekiel's Vision of Hope for Marriages*, and you will read some of my personal story as well as the stories of others who share how the Father is giving out a call in this age, for this time, to rescue His people from not just divorce that seems to be growing in leaps and bounds in our society, but from brokenness and damage to family life in many forms—from the sorrow of bereavement to the relentless pain of addictions.

We, whose story you see on these pages, who have had the privilege of this amazing rescue and healing want to share with you some very good news: The Father has an awesome plan for your recovery! It is His dream for your life.[5]

In the following chapters, you will see that while *Ezekiel's Vision of Hope for Marriages* is a call to the shepherds of this age; it is even more a challenge to everyone wanting to know they are a sheep of His pasture. Some of us *long* to be the "sheep of His pasture," but have no idea *how to find* the pasture. The message of Ezekiel is for a hurting and broken world of today; with shepherds leading the sheep to the healing pasture, and sheep sharing the good news with other sheep.[6]

You may not have spent much time in this fascinating Old Testament Book of Ezekiel, but I challenge you to spend a little time reflecting on the verses I will share with you. The answer to the challenges set forth by Ezekiel has always been the Shepherd, Jesus. You can almost hear the Father speaking through the prophet saying, "Don't make Me come down there"—but with the growing number of broken lives and broken families, it is time to hear that our Lord God *has* come down, and He is still serious about recovering His people. If you are one of His children, you can count on it.

HE MEANS BUSINESS

If you carry on with how you have been thinking in the past, you will get the same results. If you carry on doing what you have been *doing* in the past, you will get the same results. *You know* if you are ready to do whatever it takes to come into the life He planned for you from the beginning of time. You're tired of anxiety attacks and the angst in the pit of your stomach.

The good news is that God is serious about providing a personal recovery plan that will bring you and your family into freedom such as you have never, ever experienced. It is a way that demands your whole life and no compromise. If you have lived in the "far country," that state of mind full of messed up people self-helping each other, then be assured there is another way to recovery.

Let me encourage you; you, too, have a story, and I pray that someday it will be a testimony of what the Lord has done. Pray for the Father's revelation for your life. This isn't a book to tell you what to do, but rather stories and challenges that encourage you to be open to what the Holy Spirit wants to do in your life. You are His masterpiece, His workmanship, and it is for freedom that Jesus came to set you free to be all you were made to be.[7]

BUT WHY EZEKIEL?

The challenge of Ezekiel is the challenge of a prophet declaring that the Lord has something to say about how we are to live during the time when we need recovery. Take some quiet time to start reading this Old Testament book. You will see that this prophet is speaking directly to the people of God and to His shepherds. Ezekiel is a prophet who has something to say to people in pain. He is searching for people who are ready to get radical, ready to not care so much what others think but desperate to hear what Almighty God has to say about broken families and broken individuals.

We must understand Ezekiel if we are to understand what Jesus has in mind when it comes to recovery and healing of broken hearts and crushed spirits. As you read the following chapters, you will see the impact of this Old Testament prophet for New Testament living.

Ezekiel Recovery sets out a recovery challenge that is far more than you have ever imagined, for yourself if you are recovering from trauma such as divorce or suffering in the midst of family estrangement and breakdown, and for your church as it desires to be obedient to the teaching of our powerful Father God.

An Ezekiel Recovery Challenge is not in any way something you can do without the guidance of the Holy Spirit; when you take quiet time to be still and know and test that it is Him you are hearing, you will walk in the freedom that was planned for you since the beginning of time.

When your heart is broken, the world has no answers for you. Time does not heal. When you are truly ready for healing that is complete in spirit, soul, and body, then find a quiet place, get your Bible, a note book for jotting down anything that you hear from your Father, and anything you read that makes this journey personal for you—and begin!

Chapter 3

WHAT IT TAKES TO BE HEALED

Now this was the sin of your sister Sodom: She and her daughters were arrogant, overfed and unconcerned; they did not help the poor and needy. They were haughty and did detestable things before Me. Therefore I did away with them as you have seen (Ezekiel 16:49-50).

Carrie (not her real name) was born in a small town in southern England. Her mother, Jenny, loved to bake and her father, David, was a gentle man. David was the local vicar (pastor) and enjoyed talking and visiting with just about everyone in town. He was proud of his daughters, all three of them. To give Carrie's mother a break from the children (and to clear the kitchen), David would frequently take "his girls" on visiting rounds with him. To everyone in town, this looked like the ideal, loving Christian family.

It never occurred to Carrie's father that his wife was "not that keen on children." It never occurred to Carrie's mother that her husband was more than proud of his Scottish heritage when it came to saving money. These two attitudes of her parents caused unmentionable tension in Carrie—that her mother never show her love (she would scream at Carrie when no one was around to "get out of the kitchen!"), and she had no idea how to ask her father for a new pair of shoes. She saw her mother manipulate her father to meet all the family needs, and she paid attention when her mother said, "Men just don't understand that children need clothes."

As a teenager, Carrie learned that she had not been looked after very well as a baby; in fact, she had been abandoned in her crib for hours on end. As each new daughter was born right after the other, members of the congregation began to notice that Jenny would spend hours baking cakes or pies for members of their community, but would forget to nurse a baby. There never seemed to be any baby clothes, and Jenny didn't seem to have maternity clothes that fit. Some of the ladies in the church started stopping by their home at feeding time, and would hold Carrie or a little sister in a rocking chair in the corner of the kitchen while her mother baked away. Donations of clothes were warmly welcomed by Jenny and she shyly let it be known among those she trusted that David wasn't providing for her. She began to bake special pies for anyone who would give her clothes to wear. David always seemed happy to see that she had been given clothes or items for the house, especially when it didn't mean a penny out of his pocket.

As a little girl, Carrie loved trying on the new clothes the church ladies gave her. She would twirl in the vestibule of the sanctuary on Sundays to show the fine dresses or new shoes or something sparkly for her hair. Carrie loved the attention she was getting from the church family.

The first time David spanked Carrie, when she was three years old, had to do with losing some money he had put on his desk. The first time Jenny hit Carrie was when David said he would be away for a three day conference, and he hadn't remembered to leave any grocery money. Carrie's mother started hitting her, and only her, as the other children learned how to hide. Whenever the hitting began, the lashings with a broom or bat lasted an undeterminable time. Silence became the unbearable foretelling of violence. Carrie never knew exactly when her mother's beating would begin or end, but it would always be when her father left the house.

Carrie also knew not to tell her father what was going on. When he came home from a trip or a church conference, he headed straight for his study. He made it clear he didn't want to know Carrie's complaints and threatened to "beat her again" if she had done something to upset her mother. As part of reinforcing discipline, she was nine when Carrie's father started making her watch while he spanked one of her little sisters. "It will teach you what not to do!" he said. While the younger sisters were safe with their mother, they were not safe from the beatings of their father. Carrie felt helpless to rescue the young siblings she loved.

Carrie also knew that she could not share what was going on with anyone at church. She was the pastor's daughter, and as it was often said, they were to set an example for the church. They had their pride. They needed to be the perfect family, with a mother who baked for afternoon tea, a father who gave good sermons, and three perfectly behaved children. Even as she grew older and there was a youth leader who reached out to Carrie, who tried to get to know her and give her opportunities to "be real about growing up in a fishbowl," yet Carrie did not trust anyone with the truth about her family.

LONGING FOR LOVE

Longing for love and affection, Carrie started dating as early as possible to escape from the house. When she became pregnant, there was no question about whether or not to have an abortion; she would have one to save the good name of her family. Embarrassing her father would bring the whole family to shame; and in some small part of her heart, she still hoped parental love would break through. She knew by then the hatred her mother had for her father, but Carrie didn't want to add to the anger and tension that filled their home. She went for the abortion on her own. Not even her sisters knew.

In despair of ever rescuing her sisters from the verbal and physical violence that continued to fill their home, Carrie attended a university as far from home as possible. She had argued and fought her mother for as long as she could. She discussed religion with her father, but never found a truth that would stop the silence. She yearned for a faith that would break through to a peace that would restore her family, but finally she just left home, physically and emotionally. She argued with her sisters as she went out the door, making goodbyes more bearable.

Carrie was beautiful. Her beauty taught her how to gain what she wanted and thought she needed to survive in the world. Her education taught her to go after dreams and ambitions. Pride meant that Carrie married someone of some wealth as soon as possible; though like mother, like daughter, she had no concept of how to love her husband. She just wanted a high-paying job that would give her the money and the power to do what she wanted. She chased after this freedom.

Carrie's sisters handled their family life differently. The second sister learned to please her mother by eating anything and everything her mother baked. She became extremely overweight, but laughed along with her mother, saying "Like mother, like daughter. I have no willpower!" They indulged each other and while rolling out the pastries, talked about Carrie.

Carrie's youngest sister didn't go after a job or stay home to bake. She was like a deer in the headlamps, bewildered by her family. She knew she never wanted to marry and wasn't the least surprised when both older sisters married highly controlling men who never provided for their family, and then divorced. She preferred to do nothing. No job, no raising a family was worth it. Though her parents never divorced, something was broken inside their home and the pretence of a loving Christian family was a lie she did not want to live for yet another generation.

PIECES TO MEND

Carrie's life had been ripped and torn into pieces and it was obvious that some mending was needed to make it whole again. With each tear there was damage to the fabric of her soul. When I first heard her story, I was amazed she would even consider going back to church.

"Well," she said, drawing a deep breath, "after my divorce, when I lost everything, I didn't want to share my hurts with anyone. I just wanted somewhere quiet where I could see if God would talk to me. It was one last ditch effort, I suppose, to see if there was a God who could rescue me."

"Rescue?" I asked.

"Yes, from myself. I never was an alcoholic or addicted to drugs, but when you're going through the break-up of your family, there are several choices for assuaging the pain; I chose sex. It was my anesthetic of choice. I went after the rewards it brought me, and it was a comfort of sorts. One night, while alone in my apartment, the words came to me "For He is your Comforter." From deep in my childhood, Dad's sermons, or someone reading the Bible, I remembered that there was a Scripture that said something about "even if your mother and father abandon you," she said.[1]

The challenge with pain resulting from the breakdown of family life is that we are in great need of a comforter. When the Bible promises that the Holy Spirit will be our Comforter, we often think, at least to ourselves, *How? How can I ever be comforted in this depth of pain?*

We are torn apart. Needing comfort and desperate for a healer, we come to a point where we know beyond all doubt we cannot comfort or heal ourselves. We reach a point where all confidence in ourselves, all trust in others, is gone. There may be some prompting deep in our soul to reach out to God; but later, after what Carrie eventually told me about her childhood, I would have been surprised if she decided to attend the Divorce and Separation group.[2]

Yet, she did; she traveled for hours to join us for the meal at the start of the meeting. Carrie was always on time and seemed happy to see everyone. At the start of each evening's lesson though, you could see her visibly withdraw into her protective shell. It was almost as if she was another person, sitting quietly to listen to the brief talk. In our small group, she did not join in the discussions—until one night.

In about the fourth week of our meetings, Carrie spoke up. "I have something to say," she began. "You," and she pointed to Josh, one of the young men in our group, "you seem to smile now. And you," she pointed to someone else, "you seem to have some peace about your life."

Carrie then pointed to me, "And you, you aren't as quiet as you were at the start. You seem to join in discussions more. You are all getting better. But not me. I'm getting worse. Last week I only held on to life by a thread. I have battled…well, thoughts that life isn't worth living. Why are you getting better and not me?"

We sat in stunned silence. I felt the Holy Spirit speaking to me, but not sure if I should say anything. The group leader noticed something in my spirit and looked at me. I nodded and looked over at Carrie who was now looking down at tightly clasped hands.

As gently as I could, I quietly said, "Do you really want to know?"

In any other circumstance I would have thought this question absurd, but I knew I needed to ask.

Tears were now streaming down her face as she said, "Yes."

"Well...it is Jesus." I held my breath, worried she would just up and bolt out of the room, but to my amazement said, "Well then...I want to know Him."

SPIRIT, SOUL, AND BODY

In First Thessalonians 5:23-24 it says, "May God Himself, the God of peace, sanctify you through and through. May your whole spirit, soul and body be kept blameless at the coming of our Lord Jesus Christ. The One who calls you is faithful and He will do it."

This is the sanctification that will bring His peace. Carrie took the first step, and she knew that she needed to know Jesus. For a pastor's daughter, this was impressive humility. She was used to looking as if she was someone with all the answers, but here she was admitting that while she could hold her own in religious circles, she didn't know Jesus.

Carrie gained a little confidence in the way the Holy Spirit was leading her out of her personal pit. A number of us spent hours with her, listening to her story, sharing meals, meeting in the pub after our class. She began to spend more time with God, praying on her long train rides to London, as well as reading Scriptures that the Holy Spirit prompted her to read.

A number of us saw her off on her final train ride back home. I talked to her about finding a church; and I must admit I tried talking her into moving to London or searching for "an alive church" where she lived, so that she could be part of a faith family that was bold to teach God's Word and bold to show His love in everyday circumstances. I felt God had started something in her, and that she would gain so much if she allowed Him to continue what He had begun. She said she would "think about it" and see what she "felt like when she got home." Though we shared contact details, it would be a long time before we ever saw each other again.

Carrie, like all of us sitting in that group, had to make a decision to continue to be led by the Holy Spirit way past time in a class discussion. Only the Holy Spirit truly knew the damage done to our spirits and what it would take to be healed. Only the Holy Spirit could teach our spirits how to get our emotions to follow the lead of the Holy Spirit, not allowing our emotions, our feelings, to lead us, dragging us around in bondage.

THE CHOICE

Carrie hadn't been sure she "felt like" carrying on in her journey to full restoration. It's not that she didn't want to be healed; but she considered it enough, for the moment, just to know she was "saved." She was just glad to finally know beyond doubt that there was a God. As we parted at the train station, I silently prayed that someday she would want "more." She was given contact details for ministry and professional counseling, but at the moment she wasn't interested.

On the other hand, Carrie knew that I was about to drop everything—quit work and stop whatever I was doing to take time out for a full-time focus on emotional recovery from all that had happened as my family fell apart.

"All the best," she said to me. "Hope you find what you are searching for. You are brave!"

"Or crazy!" we laughed, but I just knew there had to be more to all this healing and restoration that the Bible promised. I wanted more.

THE DECISION FOR RECOVERY

Many young people take a year out from their studies to have a work experience or travel to foreign lands. I wrote about this type of "Gap Year" in my first book entitled, *Parents on the Move!*[3] As my church recovery group finished our last class together, I sensed Father God was challenging me to me to go deeper into my search for emotional healing. I was to take a "Stand in the Gap Year" for healing and restoration.

I wanted to learn how to stand on His promises and then meet Him in the gap that contained the brokenness in my life. I longed for the freedom of taking this "time out," but at first I raised every sensible obstacle. He met every one of my concerns. He provided the finances (the biggest miracle I thought at the time) and then provided the next steps for what I now refer to as "my recovery sabbatical."

I had so many questions for the Lord, and was desperate to find some answers.

There is a song in the old Baptist Hymnal, written in 1834 by Henry Lyte, called "Praise, My Soul, The King of Heaven."[4] It talks about praising God, as we are "ransomed, healed, restored, forgiven." But even if we as Christians know we are His, where and when do we *know* we are healed, forgiven, restored? What is it going to take? These questions would form the core of my sabbatical search.

Almost immediately, I found that the short answer to these questions is that my healing may be a long journey. When a family falls apart, as mine did in divorce, or we have a crisis on our hands as again, as mine did when one of our children was diagnosed with cancer, we start the healing process by accepting we can't fix our situation in a microwave moment.

Through the leading of Jesus Christ, I was given an opportunity for a sabbatical healing journey. Jesus challenged me, urged me, prompted me through the pokings of the Holy Spirit to take up the challenge of leaving all behind and seeking Him for restoration. As door after door of opportunity opened, I decided to take Him at His Word and take this time to focus on Him.

I made the decision, the commitment to healing for myself and for my whole family.

Although it has been a challenge beyond my capability, I have seen the faithfulness of God's hand and guidance as He has brought, and is bringing, restoration to all whom I love. It is no exaggeration to say this was and is an impossible dream; but it was His dream more than mine. In my humanness, I would have walked away from this dream long ago. I give thanks He brought me back to His dream every time.

Chapter 4

LET THE SABBATICAL BEGIN!

I will bring them out from the nations and gather them from the countries (Ezekiel 34:13).

Morning and evening, week after week, I drove along a back country lane to a Christian retreat center, referring to the scene before me as "the movie version of England." The flowers, the village green, the old pub, cricket being played on some summer evenings; all were on my daily drive-by. There were sheep in the fields and horses in the pastures, a little river where boys in summer shorts and girls in summer dresses, alongside the family dog, jumped in and screamed with delight. Kids were playing Pooh Sticks, and young mothers sat on green grass with blankets and homemade sandwiches. My drive continued along the stretch of trees that reminded me I was in the deep forest county of Surrey, and in the middle of this was the Great Hall and campus of Ellel Ministries Pierrepont.[1]

Knowing that I needed to go deeper into an understanding of God's plan for my life if I was ever going to *be* emotionally healthy, I signed myself up for ten weeks of classes that included teaching on Christian healing and prayer ministry.[2] I had a taste of what the Holy Spirit could do in healing the hurts of my past, and I wanted "more." I decided to take time out for a sabbatical of sorts, to sort out my life. I needed to take my "Martha personality"[3] and have some "Mary time." I needed and wanted a serious amount of time at the feet of Jesus to see what He would say, to hear His words of comfort, to hear what He wanted me to do concerning my damaged and broken family. After twenty-seven years of marriage and two wonderful children, my husband and I just about slaughtered each other on the battlefield of an unequally yoked relationship.[4] I needed time out in the wilderness, physically and spiritually.

Ellel Pierrepont is the nondenominational teaching "hospital" for emotional healing, started by Peter Horribin over twenty years ago to support pastors, church leaders (denominational and nondenominational); and quite simply, Christians from all over the world. Ellel Ministries now has four sites in the United Kingdom (one in Scotland featuring retreats for burnt-out pastors), two in Australia, one in the United States, Holland, France, Hungary, and South Africa as well and supporting ministries in Sweden, Singapore, and Taiwan. I chose to focus the first part of my recovery sabbatical in England, at the Pierrepont campus.

Jill Southern Jones is Director of Ellel Pierrepont, and it is said that once you attend her courses you are "never, ever the same."[5]

I was counting on it.

SITTING IN PEACE

While I longed to be a Mary, sitting in peace at the feet of Jesus, I had to admit I arrived at the gates of Pierrepont more as the "woman at the well,"[6] needing to meet a Savior who had living water. I was in need of a cool, long drink so I would never thirst again. I may not have had five husbands, but I needed to hear Him speak into my past, sort out the religious issues in my mind, and tell me of my hope and future with Him. I had had sips of this living water at my church and in times of prayer ministry, but now I wanted the long drink. I wanted Him to fill my cup with His living water, and I wanted more than a sip. I wanted to drink!

The classes had been going for a few weeks when one morning a member of the Pierrepont teaching team introduced her lecture with these words, "As you can see from your notes today, we will be looking at the topic of anger. While the first part of this teaching will be taken up with looking at what Father God has to say about anger in His Word, this afternoon will be a practical session where you may choose to vent some anger. You may have already discovered anger in yourselves, or there may be some anger that begins to rise up in you as we go through today's notes."[7]

With a smile, the teacher continued, "There will be bubble wrap to jump on in one room, and Styrofoam sticks to use outside to vent wrath. Scream at the top of your lungs. Stamp and stomp! There will be quite a selection of venting activities from which you may choose, including tearing up old telephone books. Have at it!" She took a deep don't-miss-this-opportunity breath and concluded, "This will be a safe place for you to express your anger!"

No wonder people said the English taught their children that wars had been won and lost on the playing fields of England. And though this teacher spoke in a soothing, if not elegant English accent, the picture she was painting of how the day would go was my worst nightmare!

I *did not* think this would be fun.

If this class was going to be a safe place for all these emotionally damaged people (who had gone through experiences at least as traumatic as mine) to vent their anger, then I wanted out of there!

Too much of my life had already been filled with people who thought *I was a safe place for them to vent their anger* and it had made life not very safe for me. Even now I froze at the thought of my past.

Thankfully, there must have been something in my student profile that alerted one of the staff members on the Ellel prayer ministry team to come and find me that morning during the "anger class." A kindly and mature woman quietly came to my desk where I sat frozen, white knuckles grasping the desk. "Would you like to go outside and take a walk?" she gently asked.

I would indeed.

They had the wisdom and experience to recognize that I was far from being at a stage where I was able to be angry. With gentleness and unconditional love, they assisted my small steps that would need to come way before I could take the giant step of recognizing that I was like Carrie's younger sister. I was the deer in the headlights—stunned by past violence, taken by surprise that Christians could have abuse in marriage.

Violence, sexual and emotional abuse was not something I had found possible to discuss. I had not told anyone, but they, the staff at Ellel, sensed and knew I had a lot to learn before I could handle deep anger, before I could recognize or comprehend what it meant to be sabotaged by a victim spirit, before I could determine just how I would do "righteous anger," and before I broke the lie that all I did was ineffectual.

Victims of violence are often most frightened of the silences and the build up of the atmospheric pressure right before the storm. Those moments, moments when others could take in teaching, were when I froze. If I had even tried to listen to the teaching, those would be the moments my heart would liken to the words used when I was told that no food would bought for me that week to eat.

Time does not heal you of this fear.

The world has no answers.

TOO ANGRY

Anna, her name was Anna, took me outside. We sat on the bench by the Great Hall door. She just let me cry. She put her safe arm around me and we sat in the summer afternoon.

As days of walking by the river or looking at the flowers or sitting quietly with my Bible turned into weeks, I allowed myself to think back about that anger class, as I called that study unit. I silently listened to stories of my classmates and the fun they recalled in tearing up phone books and stomping on plastic bubbles. Over lunch they regaled each other with "just how angry" they had been that day and how much better they felt creating havoc in the beautiful corridors of Pierrepont.

Maybe I'm just too angry, I thought. *Maybe I'm frightened of my own anger.*

Too angry to go to the supermarket, in case I tell the checkout girl how to rearrange "her supermarket" and give her a few lessons on what service should be like!

Too angry to go to church, in case I tell the pastor about a few sermons he *should* be preaching!

Too angry to have a healthy marriage, in case I lose again.

Too angry to see friends this afternoon. They'll see my anger!

Anna, my wise counselor, prayed for me. I had several personal ministry appointments with Anna and another prayer warrior named Pam. At last, a little courage came, and I began to let Father God know "just how I felt."

Outside of class, I would say things. Snippy little remarks. Do things and not do things that made all those around me uncomfortable. Oh, I could "do an Elisha!"[8] In other words, I could do huge things for Jesus and then fall apart at the small comment of a friend.

"I am *so* angry," I began to say to Father God. "I am *so* upset!" And then with head down hiding, I was appalled and ashamed that I couldn't seem to control my emotions. "So much for the Holy Spirit being in me," I despaired, "some self-control I have!"

"And just what do I do with this anger now?" I prayed in a none too holy a fashion. "What can I do with this anger?" I prayed, but I was really still asking *myself* and others.

I thought back to the anger class. Where were the old phonebooks? Would it help to tear them? What would it be like to let it rip? I heard about a room at Ellel in Australia where, while attending what they call The Understanding Anger Day, you could throw plates a la Greek Taverna style! That sounded more like it.

I found plates I didn't like, and I smashed them all, and I smashed them right out the back door of my house. I smiled at neighbors and said, "Don't mind me, I'm taking an anger course. Class assignment."

But the anger didn't disappear.

After I completed part one of the course, I took a vacation to Florida. While relaxing and going over in my mind some of the concepts I had learned at Pierrepont, I realized the feeling that I associated with anger was at it again, rising up, and welling up within. *Oh no*, I thought, *helpless as the dark cloud rolled in. I'm out of plates that I want to donate to this cause. Father God, what can I do?!*

Swimming instantly came to mind. That's what I would do. I would vent all this emotional energy by pounding up and down the pool. Maybe by the time I did a few laps, I could feel like being a nice person, or at least not bite the mailcarrier.

Swim suit on, quick one-minute walk to the pool. In I went. Back and forth, back and forth, swimming to and fro. *OK, Lord, see me here, trying to be angry and not sin.*

I was fed up with comfort eating, fed up lashing out with criticism, fed up trying to get this anger out and not sin.

I bashed back and forth the lanes of the pool. Finally I admitted, *Lord, it's not working.*

I stood straight up and looked at the clear blue sky, so thankful to have the pool to myself.

And that's when I heard the Holy Spirit say, "It's not anger."

What do you mean it's not anger?! I was indignant. *Isn't this what it feels like?*

I had been so long in the denial lane of life, and I thought I had made progress in overcoming the "scared to be there" lane, what on earth could this pent-up emotion be?

Instantly there was a check in my spirit that said, "Ask Him."

"OK, Father…" But almost before I could ask the question, the Holy Spirit said, "It's self-pity."

I was mortified. How embarrassing.

THE LAST PARTY

It was Father God's gracious love that tumbled down into my mind and my heart, enabling me to bear hearing Him say, "But you *need to get angry.* You need to get very angry and take authority over what the enemy has stolen from you and even now is trying to steal."

His words in my heart *continued* to roll down like thunder into my understanding, thoughts almost tripping over each other:

"When you act out of self-pity you easily sin; when you act out of the lie that you are ineffectual, you easily sin; when you act out of feeling powerless to change situations, you easily sin; but when you are warring against the enemy, you will know what righteous anger obtains—freedom to come closer to the Father, and in that place you are more than safe. In that place you have peace that passes understanding. Everything changes when you are in the shelter of your Father."

I went over to the side of the pool—too shocked to swim. Before I could argue or allow protest to rise up in myself, I set my course: No more pity parties. No more. I'm done. I couldn't live like this anymore. I was destroying myself and all that was around me.

I felt like the last one left after a very large and out-of-control party, and it was way past midnight. In my mind I wasn't at the pool edge, but sitting on a chair with streamers all around me, dirty plates stacked high, glasses and bottles all over the place, and I was the one-woman, clean-up committee. I pictured myself blowing on a little horn and sitting back in the party chair. This wasn't going to be fun—cleaning up the mess in my mind—and I was tired just thinking about it.

I stayed with this mental picture and looked all around me and my big, party, wedding tent, a white marquee for my "self-pity party" extended way back across the lawn into childhood; in fact, I could see that this party had been going on for a few generations.

In my mind, I pictured myself sitting motionless at one of the tables. "So, Lord," I said, "how do I clean up this mess?"

"We." He said.

"We?" *Now there was hope! Was God going to come and clean all this up for me? Could this be the ball of wool I toss on His lap?*

He read my mind. "I will do My bit and you can do yours."

"Oh," I said crestfallen. Now I was looking around for the large black bags and thinking what sort of stain removal might work on those beautiful, white linen tablecloths.

Gently He said, "Have you ever wanted to pick up a tablecloth off one of those round banquet tables and just dump the whole thing?"

I nodded. Like right now. "But, what about the beautiful china? These aren't paper plates I had at my party." I recalled my extravagant retail therapy.

"Look again," He said, "They are mostly all smashed."

I pictured standing up and going to a table or two. There the fine china and beautiful tea cups that showed no expense was spared, in pieces. I looked at Jesus.

"I'll be outside," He said.

"You aren't leaving me with this mess are You?" I said sadly, looking at one rather large table that had a little engraved sign on it, "Pity party for every aspect of your former marriage and divorce." So many people had sat with me at that table. They had said I had had every right to a little self-pity.

There were so many tables representing events or things said and done to me. When I should have been angry, instead I thought I had no choice but to feel helpless, a victim, settling down into the crushing of my spirit.

"When you are ready to pick up the four corners of that tablecloth, just bundle it all together and come outside. I'll be there by the cross. You can just dump it," He said.

I nodded. The cross would never come inside the pity party marquee. I would have to drag out the debris myself. "Lead me by the tables," I said to Jesus. "I don't want to miss any."

And so my Brother, my Friend, my Savior came with me to a table or two and though I had my hands around the mess, He actually carried the load and only took His hands away when we got to the cross— and then I had to let go for the bundle to drop.

What seemed like hours but what were only minutes later, I finally stood up and wrapped the beach towel around me. I looked down at the pool. I knew in a heartbeat that I didn't need to deal with every messed up table in my life right at that moment. There was a fleeting pinch of discouragement as I pictured a lot of "dragging and dropping to do," but He swiftly reminded me of the table He was preparing for overcomers[9] and that table would be better than anything I set for myself.

If I think no expense had been spared at my pity parties, then I needed to think about a table where He had every resource available to Father, Son, and Holy Spirit. No eye had seen, and no mind had even imagined what the Father has planned for us.

By His mercy, you and I are invited.

Chapter 5

FORGIVENESS

Because they lead My people astray, saying "Peace," when there is no peace, and because, when a flimsy wall is built, they cover it with whitewash... (Ezekiel 13:10).

The BBC newscaster was desperate not to smile as he related the story on the nine o'clock news reporting the adventure of "Lady Sarah Graham Moon and Revenge in the Village.[1] It seems this true story starts with the lord of the manor in this still feudal village frequenting the local pub. His lordship enjoyed a pint or two, alongside the serving girl. They began an affair. The lady of the manor went about her business, arranging flowers at the local church and assisting those less fortunate. Those who frequented the pub began to talk and speculate as to whether or not her ladyship actually knew what was going on. They were to soon see that she knew very well what was going on—but was, well, a lady. One weekend, his lordship and the serving girl went away "on business." Now eyebrows were raised all over that village.

Early one morning her ladyship paid a visit to the milkman; but before you think I am even suggesting any impropriety, let me assure you that she was simply asking him if he would stop by the manor and then let her accompany him on his rounds, delivering milk to each house. And so before dawn, her ladyship and the milkman placed a bottle of milk and one of the finest wines from his lordship's cellar to each and every doorstep. Oh, and each of these vintage delights had a little jacket—a sleeve from his lordship's designer suits.

The following Sunday, her ladyship attended the village church as usual, but smiles replaced raised eyebrows on the pews that day—or at least, that is how I heard the story.

Over the course of my recovery sabbatical I heard many stories. As part of my personal journey, I listened to stories and I wrote stories; but always Father God seemed to be drawing me in to learning from my own story and sharing personal stories with others. He seemed to be taking every thread of my life and weaving a new story for my life.

One of the things Father God had me do during my recovery sabbatical was to use my teacher training from previous years to review what I learned at Ellel.[2] There is nothing like teaching to get you to think about what you have learned! Weeks after my wonderful time at Pierrepont, I was asked to share something of what I learned with a women's group. My church also had me use some of the material from my original recovery course,[3] and I had the opportunity to teach on Family Recovery for Christians in both the United States and in England.

In these groups, we looked at stories concerning forgiveness—or not forgiving, as the case may be. I always asked if anyone wanted to share what they did, or didn't do, or would have liked to have done "in vengeance," before becoming prepared to even think about forgiveness for damage in their personal family life. We shared these stories in confidence; and though it was to our total embarrassment, we always had a good laugh. These stories were not funny, but oh we have laughed until we cried upon hearing them.

Then we recalled whether or not our church family was "there for us" at the time our families fell apart. That wiped the smile off most faces. Many said their church was "not there for them." Some said, they knew their church might have wanted to help, or did help materially, but just did not have the training to help with what had been referred to as "domestic issues."

"I was too much to handle," I heard from course participants again and again.

"They [church leaders] were scared to get involved."

"No one wanted to take sides."

"They wondered at the legal implications."

"There was too much going on at church already to even think about assisting me prevent a possible divorce."

Many Christians tell stories of feeling they had to leave their church when their family fell apart; it was just all too much for the congregation, and they couldn't handle the shame.

Then I asked, "Did anyone go looking for you? Anyone call you to find out where you were? Anyone come after you who was *equipped* to help?"

TIME OUT

Through the teaching and ministry of the highly trained Ellel prayer team, I gained insights that helped me get back into normal church life. In this year-long sabbatical, which I started in what Peter Horribin calls a "teaching hospital" for emotional healing,[4] I took time out to get a focus on following Jesus in a healing journey.

I took time to renounce self-pity. I had a humiliating "victim spirit" lifted off me. I cut off and shut off any spirit of offense that would land in my mind, and blocked giving the enemy a landing pad for work in my life. I likened *thoughts* of revenge-due-to-anger as flights into the runway-strip of my mind. I learned *how* to shut down the airport.

Next was a life lesson about the armor of God. I already knew the verses in Ephesians 6:10.

I put on the belt of truth. It is by truth that all other pieces of the armor connect. I put on the breast plate, acknowledging but not yet grasping that the breastplate would conform me to righteousness, getting right with God.

I put on the shoes of the Gospel of Good News, and asked Father God, through the teachings of Jesus and the still small voice of the Holy Spirit, to guide my footsteps daily. Then I picked up the sword, which is the Word of God, and His Word would teach me what and how to battle. I "got it," that it is with His Word we do battle.

Then I put on the helmet of salvation, so thankful that there was protection in salvation for my mind, eyes, ears, and mouth. At last I picked up the shield. I would raise the shield whenever fiery darts of words that could hurt me came near, whether in words from others or words of self-talk.

I stood there in my armor in one of my training sessions with one of the most amazing prayer warriors I have ever known. Her name is Judy.

JUDY

"Nice set of armor," said Judy in her straightforward Canadian-British way. Judy is dual national, but as part of Ellel's teaching team, it's God's Kingdom she is passionate about, whether she is praying with the former leaders of the Lord's Resistance Army in the Sudan[5] or helping someone like me, a pitifully helpless-at-that-time divorcee who is "twice southern."

Twice southern is an accolade given to me by my maternal grand-mother when she heard I was marrying someone from England. To her, the deep south of Southern Baptist America was the only place that knew true manners.

"Oh well," my grandmother said, "at least you are marrying someone from Southern England. You'll be twice southern."

"This southern politeness has gotta go," said Judy. It was driving her crazy.

"Come on," she said, "get some backbone. I want you to stand here and out loud tell the enemy to get off!"

I tried.

Judy didn't laugh. "Try again."

I tried again.

"Come on, Kathleen! Declare what you want to say to the enemy...do not invite him for a conversation and mint juleps! Get some Holy Spirit like they have in Texas in you!"

I was louder this time.

"It's not about louder. It's about meaning it!"

Again, I told the enemy where to go. Judy took my hand, "You can do this, Kathleen."

"No I can't."

"Yes, you can."

"No, I can't."

"OK," she said. "Just let the enemy have your life then. Roll over and let him have everything precious to you."

I thought he already had everything. My marriage. My kids' relationship with me. My home.

Judy read my mind. "You can fight a very good fight. Take a stand. When you have done everything you can do, stand. Stand before the Lord your God and tell Him the desire of your heart. But tell the enemy to go. Tell! Don't ask! Tell the enemy that you are serving the Lord Jesus Christ ONLY and he, the enemy, is to get his hands off your kids!"

That I did.

"Finally!" said Judy. And then she hugged me and something was healed—though what was healed I did not know at that moment.

ANOTHER SOUTHERN

And then it happened. God was ready to speak to me.

In an awesome moment that I will never forget, another southern, this time Jill Southern Jones, head of Pierrepont, stood before the Never Ever the Same (NETS) class.[6] "Get out your Bibles," she said, "and turn with me to Ezekiel 34. I am going to read it to you in entirety, the whole chapter."

OK. We turned to the chapter in our Bibles, some of us struggling to find verses we had rarely found useful.

She started to read. One sentence, two verses, three verses, and I was blown away. I couldn't read silently along with Jill. I closed my eyes. Tears streamed down my face as the words poured into my spirit. I was ruined as I listened to her words. Ruined for life with these life changing words that showed me that I couldn't even begin to dream up the level of anger Father God had on my behalf. He would teach me what anger looked like, and I couldn't even touch it, match it, do anything but stand in awe that the Creator of Life was passionate about me. You do not mess with His children.

This is what she read:

Ezekiel 34:

The Word of the Lord came to me:

"Son of man, prophesy against the shepherds of Israel; prophesy and say to them: 'This is what the Sovereign Lord says: Woe to the shepherds of Israel who only take care of themselves! Should not shepherds take care of the flock?

You eat the curds, clothe yourselves with the wool and slaughter the choice animals, but you do not take care of the flock. You have not strengthened the weak or healed the sick or bound up the injured. You have not brought back the strays or searched for the lost. You have ruled them harshly and brutally.

So they were scattered because there was no shepherd, and when they were scattered they became food for all the wild animals. My sheep wandered over all the mountains and on every high hill. They were scattered over the whole earth, and no one searched or looked for them.

"'Therefore, you shepherds, hear the word of the Lord: As surely as I live, declares the Sovereign Lord, because My flock lacks a shepherd and so has been plundered and has become food for all the wild animals, and because My shepherds did not search for My flock but cared for themselves rather than

for My flock, therefore O shepherds, hear the word of the Lord: This is what the Sovereign Lord says; I am against the shepherds and I will hold them accountable for My flock. I will remove them from tending the flock so that the shepherds can no longer feed themselves. I will rescue My flock from their mouths, and it will no longer be food for them.

"'For this is what the Sovereign Lord says: I Myself will search for My sheep and look after them. As a shepherd looks after his scattered flock when he is with them, so will I look after My sheep. I will rescue them from all the places where they were scattered on a day of clouds and darkness. I will bring them out from the nations and gather them from the countries, and I will bring them into their own land. I will pasture them on the mountains of Israel, in the ravines and in all the settlements in the land. I will tend them in a good pasture, and the mountain heights of Israel will be their grazing land. There they will lie down in good grazing land, and there they will feed in a rich pasture on the mountains of Israel. I Myself will tend My sheep and have them lie down, declares the Sovereign Lord. I will search for the lost and bring back the strays. I will bind up the injured and strengthen the weak, but the sleek and the strong I will destroy. I will shepherd the flock with justice.

"'As for you, My flock, this is what the Sovereign Lord says: I will judge between one sheep and another, and between rams and goats. Is it not enough for you to feed on the good pasture? Must you also trample the rest of your pasture with your feet? Is it not enough for you to drink clear water? Must you also muddy the rest with your feet? Must My flock feed on what you trampled and drink what you have muddied with your feet?

"'Therefore this is what the Sovereign Lord says to them: See, I Myself will judge between the fat sheep and the lean sheep. Because you shove with flank and shoulder, butting all the weak sheep with your horns until you have driven them away, I will save My flock and they will no longer be plundered. I will judge between one sheep and another. I will place over them one shepherd, My servant David, and he will tend them, he will tend

them and be their shepherd. I the Lord will be their God, and My servant David will be their prince among them. I the Lord have spoken.

"'I will make a covenant of peace with them and rid the land of wild beasts so that they may live in the desert and sleep in the forests in safety. I will bless them and the places surrounding My hill. I will send down showers in season; there will be showers of blessing. The trees of the field will yield their fruit and the ground will yield its crops; the people will be secure in their land. They will know that I am the Lord, when I break the bars of their yoke and rescue them from the hands of those who enslaved them. They will no longer be plundered by the nations, nor will wild animals devour them. They will live in safety, and no one will make them afraid. I will provide for them a land renowned for its crops, and they will no longer be victims of famine in the land or bear scorn of the nations. Then they will know that I, the Lord their God, am with them and that they, the house of Israel, are My people, declares the Sovereign Lord, You My sheep, the sheep of My pasture, are people, and I am your God, declares the Sovereign Lord.'"

And you haven't seen anger if you haven't seen how angry our Father is when the Church doesn't go after and rescue or become equipped to seek after one of His kids. If you are His, He is passionate about you. If I wanted to learn about anger, I had come to the master. We can't even grasp the basic meaning of anger until we see just how angry He is about anyone messing with the children of the living Lord.

As Jill Southern Jones finished her reading she said, "And no one goes in the Too Hard Basket. That's the basket where churches put people who seem to be too much of a challenge for healing, and where binding up wounds doesn't fit in with Wednesday night prayer meeting.

"Some of you have allowed yourselves to be put into that basket by your church, by your family…some of you have even put yourselves there," she said, and to this day I believe she looked straight at me.

"Even me, Lord. I have to get out of this basket," I prayed. I sat quietly at my desk at the end of class that day, stunned by His anger on my behalf, amazed at the passion of His love.

THE GARDEN

After class I went for a walk in the woods, my little wilderness, and in my mind I could see Jesus in a garden. Not the perfect Garden of Eden, but the one at Gethsemane. I could picture Him. It was a hot July day (and yes, I was in England), but for me it was Easter. So powerful He was, on His knees talking to the Father and praying breakthrough to eternity for me, for the disciples falling asleep, for everyone who had let me down—so we could all have life.

And then I could see it: I needed to get angry at anything that would keep me from this life for which He died. Words that I hardly understood but were surprisingly fierce in my spirit came to my mind, "Nothing was to keep me from a life in the Kingdom. I was to have a place at His table."

Though I made note of these words, at the moment I was more excited that *I got* it about God being angry on my behalf, jealous for me. Just knowing that the results of a righteous God, angry on my behalf, *would produce results* way beyond any temper tantrum I could have about life being unfair, I knew that I was ready to start the hard work of learning what I had heard called "spiritual warfare."

Just knowing God's passion about my protection, my recovery, and my having all I need to live life in freedom meant I was in a safe place; safe to learn about anger, safe to have this new kind of fight for all that was precious to me. Up until this point in my life, it seemed the enemy always won.

WHEN IT'S NOT SO EASY

Through the teaching at Pierrepont, I began to understand, with profound gratitude, that Father God was serious about my rescue from the pit of a life not being lived. I *got it* that Jesus had died so that I could have "fullness of life," and that it was the enemy that had come to steal and destroy whatever was good about life. I now understood *how* I had opened the door to that enemy.

"Come in," I had said by virtue of not living a godly life before I was married, "you seem harmless enough."

I hadn't realized God was *serious* about what He said regarding the sanctity of marriage. *He is serious* about His Kingdom way of living. *I hadn't* taken Him that seriously; He was part of my life, but mostly as a topic of good discussion. His commandments had simply been debating points for me—and precepts to live by when having a good day. "Legalism" was the label I used for anything that smacked of guidelines for living.

But as I learned just how much He was on my side for walking in freedom from anxiety, defeat of my hopes and dreams, I started getting rid of anything that would allow the enemy any entry into my life. I cleared out rubbish books and stopped wasting time with mindless television. Mindful of not becoming too sanctimonious and a real "prig" as the English say, I dared myself to clean up the words I used, and stopped declaring negative things over my life. I would later learn about "Date Night with the Lord," but for now I just spent more time writing down verses and committing them to memory. I was desperate to get rid of feelings of shame and condemnation. I was desperate to find the power of the Holy Spirit and show the way of recovery to my children—but first *I* needed to find it!

As Father God had proved serious about loving me, and by that I mean that unconditional, committed agape love,[7] I got even more serious about my relationship with Him. So when a feeling of condemnation continued, I knew what to do. It was back to the Shepherd! I raised my "shield" by telling the enemy to "get off my mind!" so I could even think, even hear the Shepherd.

"It's that forgiveness issue again," I heard the gentle Holy Spirit say.

You will recognize people desperate for answers when they immediately read every book available about forgiving others and forgiving themselves—that was me. I *knew* that shame was all about not forgiving *myself*; so I made an uncompromising choice to forgive myself, as well as family and friends.

As I had a deep desire to learn something I could share with my children, something of God that would be of value to salvage their lives, I pressed on. I was keen to use this sabbatical to learn how we could all be restored. Important as it was to teach and develop what I was starting to see as a calling on my life, I didn't want to just teach a class on recovery ministry, *I wanted to see recovery* for all my family. This had to be real in my life.

I asked Father God again, to forgive me for divorcing my ex-husband. No excuses. I then tried to contact anyone I could to apologize for the effect my divorce had on my community, but it wasn't always possible. One of my former friends just couldn't bring herself to speak to me. I knew I needed to forgive her for not forgiving me. It was such a mess.

I longed to *feel forgiveness*. At the same time as I became more honest with myself, I realized I longed for family and friends, church family friends, to be sorry for all the hurt they had caused me, for their lack of understanding, for their not seeing I had cried for so long for help and they had not seen. They had not heard, even ignored my plea for help. I wanted them to apologize. I only had to think about my children and I despaired at what Christians had done and not done to help pull a family, my family, out of the brokenness pit.

But they were not sorry. They saw no reason to apologize. I was the one who had divorced.

"Anyway" Forgiveness

In Christian circles, we are often told to forgive anyone and everyone "anyway." You are told to "let it go." I give thanks that it wasn't long before one of the books on my sabbatical reading list was Gary Chapman's *Five Languages of Apology*.[8] In this book, Dr. Chapman states that we often ask Christians to do something that even God doesn't expect of us.

From our own experience we know that the example of Christ on the cross is often used as a story of Jesus forgiving people no matter what they have done, knowingly and unknowingly. Not true. It seems He asked *the Father* to forgive them, for they "know not what they do." He released them into what I started calling "escrow forgiveness."

Escrow Forgiveness

If we confess our sins, He is faithful and just and will forgive us or sins and purify us from all unrighteousness. If we claim we have not sinned, we make Him out to be a liar and His Word has no place in our lives (1 John 1:9-10).

Escrow is where you release money into an account, ready and waiting to be used once someone has signed on the dotted line—once someone has taken responsibility. When they do take responsibility, and you have agreement regarding the details of the transaction, that money moves swiftly into their account.

In every situation where we are struggling with forgiveness, we need to check to see if we are waiting for an apology. Some things, little things people do that irritate us, we may need to learn how to just shrug off the offense and let go. We need to remember that we all make mistakes. We need to "get over ourselves," as I hear New Yorkers say.

Sometimes we need to learn that a friend or family member has actually apologized, but we have not understood their language of apology. We might be speaking Mandarin, so to speak, and they might be speaking Welsh. As I read Gary Chapman's *Languages of Apology*, I learned a few new apology languages.

But for the more serious issues, the issues that seem to demand a reconciliation that would or could be a danger to the emotional health of all concerned, I knew I needed a deeper understanding of the example Jesus gave. Dr. Chapman reminds us that God did not make light of every issue.[9] Jesus did not go around saying, "Don't worry. Your sins are forgiven," in every case.

There were times when: No apology? No repentance? Forgiveness is right there in reach, waiting for us when we take responsibility.

On the cross, the soldiers attacking Jesus were given this escrow forgiveness, and when they took responsibility and acknowledged what they had done, forgiveness was ready and waiting. There was no unforgiveness in the heart of Jesus. They were forgiven before they asked, but when they asked they received it.[10]

A close friend of mine is the daughter of a registered sex offender. Her dad abused her relentlessly when she was growing up. It affected her, to say the least, and it was an underlying cause of not having a healthy, successful marriage. Many in her family continue to live in denial of what went on, and those who know want her to forgive her father. "After all, you are the Christian in the family," they say. My friend longs to forgive and even dares to dream that "that man" could be healed enough for her to call him "father."

However, he makes light of his behavior, and even wonders why it bothers her. He can't seem to understand why she won't "let it go!"

Unforgiveness of her father poisons her heart, but forgiveness without repentance would be a lie, and it would not be the forgiveness that opens a door to a closer relationship. God sets the example of wanting to see repentance in our hearts, so that He can forgive us. We need to humble ourselves with repentance. We need to turn from our wicked ways. We need to call on His name in truth (see Ps. 145:18).

And so, for my friend, she is in the process of taking the whole situation to the cross for a divine exchange—her damage for His healing touch. "Father God, my earthly dad doesn't seem to get it." She prays, "He doesn't seem to understand the damage he has done to me. Make me willing to be willing to forgive him, for Your name's sake. Take unforgiveness from my heart so that I am ready to forgive him when he is ready to truly repent. Father, forgive him, for he hasn't a clue."

My friend's father wants reconciliation without forgiveness; yet it is forgiveness that can begin the process of reconciliation. Repentance is not to be side-stepped.

Truth will set you free. The truth is, sometimes we need to let things go, and sometimes we need to know that the person who has sinned against us is truly sorry without hearing a word. We need to ask the Holy Spirit for His guidance, His discernment. We need to ask the Holy Spirit to tell us if there is any unforgiveness in our hearts and to make us ready and willing to forgive His way and in His time.

As we pray for the people we find a challenge to forgive, let us consider releasing forgiveness, making it ready and waiting for the time of understanding, for a time when those who sin against us realize what they did or did not do. We do not need unforgiveness to stay in our hearts where it would grow a root of bitterness, blocking us from the freedom meant for our lives. As we take forgiveness and put it at the cross, ready and waiting with our "Father they do not know what they have done," let us pray that the ones who have sinned against us receive a revelation.

Like the prodigal son who headed home, the father had already forgiven him. He ran down the road to meet his son. No word needed to be said between father and son. Who knows, maybe the father had done something to make the younger son want to leave? Maybe the brother was too difficult to live with? Who knows? Family life can be, and most times is, complicated. They both knew there was no life in the pit, and the father wanted the son to return home. Repentance and forgiveness opened a door, *the* door, for the *start* of reconciliation and restoration.

THE EZEKIEL CHALLENGE FOR TODAY

All through my recovery sabbatical, I continued to read and re-read Ezekiel. It was one of my greatest challenges to acknowledge that "forgiveness" had often been pushed on me, and I pushed it on myself. I had used forgiveness as a way of hoping that if I forgave someone, any pain I felt would just go away. Ezekiel talks about people calling for "peace, when there is no peace," and condemns those who "whitewash" over issues instead of taking an honest look at areas of our lives.

We do not have to look far to see the example of world leaders "whitewashing" over issues today. Diplomats almost trip over themselves to reach agreements with those who would do harm. Anything for a peaceful world! We do the same in our communities, and we push issues under the rug in our own homes.

Where Scripture calls for not letting the sun go down on our anger,[11] we can't begin conversations that would bring true peace in our marriages. We pull the blanket over our heads rather than say "sorry," at the end of the day.

We have to face the reality that the Lord God is just as angry today as He was in Ezekiel's time when He said:

> *They lead My people astray, saying "Peace," when there is no peace, and because, when a flimsy wall is built they cover it with whitewash. Therefore tell those who cover it* [the wall] *with whitewash that it is going to fall. I will tear down the wall you have covered with whitewash and will level it to the ground so that its foundation will be laid bare...* (Ezekiel 13:11,14).

Today we have to ask ourselves, what walls are we building? Walls for protection? Our boundaries? What walls are being built between nations, between communities, among family and friends, between husbands and wives—because we can't forgive? What and where are the cracks? Where are our walls broken? What are we whitewashing?

Where are the stupid walls we have built for ourselves? Where do we need repentance and forgiveness instead of denying issues that matter to God? Where are the walls God would build for our protection, walls on which we would have angels stand and watch?

As I asked myself these questions, I started to sense I was heading to some recovery "promised land," and even now I stand amazed at what the Father began to tell me.

RELEVANT SCRIPTURES

The following Scriptures give you the essence of how much your Father God loves you:

> *I will give you a new heart and put a new spirit in you; I will remove from you your heart of stone and give you a heart of flesh* (Ezekiel 36:26).

The Lord is near to all who call on Him, to all who call on Him in truth. He fulfills the desires of those who fear Him, He hears their cry and saves them (Psalm 145:18-19).

Jesus looked at them and said, "With man this is impossible, but with God all things are possible" (Matthew 19:26).

Chapter 6

THE WALL OF HOSTILITY

This land that was laid waste has become like the garden of Eden... (Ezekiel 36:35).

One of the biggest surprises that comes to those who have opened the "forgiveness door" is that there is suddenly a wall—and it's in your face. There it is, standing tall and seemingly insurmountable, and it seeks to trap you at every turn. It is called a Wall of Hostility.

This wall can trick you and it can break you. It's a tough wall—tall and built to last.

Josh (not his real name) had been stunned looking at the hostility wall that stood right before him as he opened the door to forgiveness with his former wife. As part of the Monday night Divorce Recovery and Separation class at Holy Trinity Brompton,[1] he learned the power of forgiveness for obtaining peace in his own life. As a strong Christian, he believed the truth of the Lord's Prayer and knew that at least eventually, unforgiveness was not an option.

"I forgave my wife, and I continue to forgive my wife," he said, "because I don't want to carry around bitterness in my mind. It's not healthy for me or for the children. We could use a little reconciliation, and you can only do that if you choose to forgive each other. Forgive and let some things go."

Josh believed that even *practicing* the concept of forgiveness was a witness to the Christian faith for his ex-wife. What he hadn't expected was the hostility that faced him at every turn.

His ex-wife didn't want forgiveness; she had little use for the Christian way of life and was hostile to even the thought of reconciliation. She had left Josh to be with another woman.

"I didn't know how to handle this. I forgave her for so many things. This forgiveness kept my heart and mind strong, but she was so hostile to anything I did or said. I wanted to have the kids, especially on weekends so they could go to church with me, but all I could count on was a growing resistance and mind games from her and her partner. It was impossible."

HOSTILE WALL WITHIN

When we first choose to forgive or to take that no-turning-back step to give our life totally to the Lord and understand we need to receive forgiveness, hitting hostility can be quite a shock. Maybe we have pride deep within that is hostile to cleansing our hearts and minds. The hostility that comes with pride shows itself by attempting to sabotage a new, uncompromising life in Christ at every turn.

There can be a war waging inside us. Thoughts breed anxiety, or fears bombard our mind, our will, and our relentless emotions. Hostility may come from others when they interpret forgiveness as arrogance as they see us forgiving them for what they have done and not done; but wherever the hostility originates, the battle to break down this wall is within.

Josh, like many of us, was fighting the hostile wall of words. Words from others, words we told ourselves. Words that came way before a spouse said, "I want a divorce," and way before words were said in the court room where justice may or may not have happened on a dark and cloudy day.[2]

The wall of hostility is also a wall of actions—actions of others and our own actions that sabotage recovery. Many of us have faced the reality that even from loved ones there have been actions that were not for our good but for our demise. Many of us have had family and friends who are not in our corner and mean us harm. Josh, like a lot of us who have experienced the breakdown of good, emotionally healthy family life (some of us have never experienced it), was saddened to face the reality of a spouse who held him not in the words of a marriage vow of honor, but contempt.

There are so many stories; and if you are reading this book with the desire to see your family whole and healed, you will have your own story. In the pit of despair you reach up to God, crying out for forgiveness and in faith longing to have a heart that will truly forgive those who hurt you. You want the hostility between you and your family members to disappear. Cease and desist!

Shame covers this hostile wall that separates you from the real you—whether you built the wall, others built the wall, or it was a team project. Shame has cried out from every brick in this wall, and our own lack of reality as well as the intrigues of men and women have made each of us feel like failures in our attempts to break it down. We *have* failed.

Most of us, after opening the door of forgiveness are shocked by what hits us. We have been frustrated by the fact that there seems to be very little we could do to make those words, the anxious thoughts, the fear go away, and the actions of others come to some good. The hostile wall just stood there, in the way of freedom and a good night's sleep.

THE ENEMY

The enemy comes only to "steal and kill, and destroy" (John 10:10). The enemy is good at creating panic attacks or getting you to live with low-grade, day in and day out anxiety. That ball of twisted pain in your stomach is one of his better tactics. The enemy's kingdom is full of stealing from your bank account, robbing you of sleep, killing ambition, and destroying friendships and relationships. Our response, especially when we aren't ready and dressed for battle, is panic! We despair and feel like we are living in a pit. It's the pit of life and it's the pit where the enemy wants you—walled in, deep in the pit.

When we get to that place in our minds where we stay on the front line of battle by recognizing that recovery from family breakdown *is* a battle, we make a decision to be overcomers. We make a decision to face the reality of the need for anger, real anger—anger that sends the enemy flying. Self-pity is a waste of time in this battle, and it keeps us from even seeing that a battle is going on, never mind the reality that we need to be learning a new style of warfare. When we choose to forgive anyone, including ourselves and anything that keeps us from living the life our Lord died to give us, then the door is open to reality—to the high and hostile wall built of hatred, which is intended to keep you out of the Kingdom of God.

The wall of hostility is the enemy's barricade to keep us from being all we were meant to be. The enemy gives the world a lot of time and money to spend to keep people thinking they can climb that wall themselves, go around it, or whitewash it; but it is misdirection all the way.

I had let the enemy steal my time by reading magazines and self-help books, joining Internet chat groups, and flicking the remote in search of magic that mislead me into thinking I could face a hostile world and succeed. He robbed me of my money in getting me to consider retail therapy or some other life-wasting addiction as a way to numb the pain from all the hostility to what I wanted to do or be. He played havoc with my desires. He destroyed my confidence and then laughed when out of low self-esteem I messed up!

I've learned that forgiveness is the absolute wild card that opens the door to what is truly going on as the enemy steals, kills, and destroys your life. What is going on is hostility to Kingdom living in the name of Jesus. That is the battle, and the truth of this will set us free to fight a real fight, not wallow in the pit. When we *get* this principle, we are free to watch and wait on the Lord—to remove the wall and have His Kingdom come!

When I saw truthfully where hostility originates, I knew where to direct the anger that fuels my training in spiritual warfare. I had to reach a point where I hate what God hates and love what He loves. Instead of striking out at the person on the bus, a neighbor, a sibling, or even, dare I say, my former or estranged spouse, I learned I could train myself to get very, very angry at the enemy. Forgive the person. Hate the enemy.

We can forgive the person, and indeed resist the enemy. "Forgiveness and resistance" is not some passive, little two-step dance. It is active and at times exhausting; but there is no other way out of the pit. We have to decide. Do we want out? Do we want our whole family free? Do we want to see our Maker tear down the wall?

We can take great rest and comfort in knowing that the forgiveness-resistance battle belongs to the Lord. That is something we need to remind ourselves in our midnight hour. It is His battle, this spiritual warfare. We forgive and continue to forgive where and when He directs us to forgive; and then we come to know deep within that He is God of our lives as we see *Him* break down the wall of hostility. In this knowing, we can begin to learn sharp and effective resistance. In awe we need to stand and watch the Master. The wildness of forgiveness keeps us working on forgiveness, whether it is a will-choice to forgive, escrow forgiveness, or the privilege of outright, pure forgiveness. It is the audacity of resistance that makes us bold.

Accepting that the battle of breaking down the hostility wall belongs to the Lord finally enables resting in Him; but as we begin to learn this next step in our Ezekiel Challenge for recovery, we see He gives us plenty to do. While the strategy and the supplies for the battle are from God, we are learning how to be His. Recovery is that incredible life combination of spa and boot camp.

THE PRISON

In the second term of my sabbatical studies in that "emotional healing teaching hospital" better known as Ellel Ministries,[3] I made an appointment for an intensive prayer ministry session. I wanted to learn the forgiveness-resistance two-step strategy.

For this personal appointment, as they called the two to three-hour session, I met with two highly trained and experienced prayer ministers, two women of God who had a passion for helping people come into Father God's freedom for their lives. We prayed together. We waited on the Lord; and as we waited, I began to have a picture of me being in a prison cell. I could see myself sitting on a bench, not moving.

At first I didn't share this picture with the prayer warriors, but I didn't need to—they already knew. One of these gentle ladies said she sensed an "imprisoned spirit," and asked "Is that right? What do you think?" I just nodded, yes. We continued to sit still and wait on the Father, to see if in His graciousness He would reveal any more to me.

One of the women asked me questions about my life, and then she asked me if the Holy Spirit was saying anything? I shared what I was thinking, not sure what was from God and what were just my soulish thoughts. Ellel Ministries is careful not to lead people into visual imagery or to feed words into people's lives that might not be God speaking. Everything is checked and confirmed and questioned. Is what we are hearing from God? If yes, it will be confirmed. I knew in my spirit we were on the right track.

As I closed my eyes and prayed, I could see the bars of the cell where I was sitting, but I couldn't move from the rough wooden bench where in my mind I sat.

"Jesus is calling you to come out of this cell, this prison, Kathleen," said one of the ladies.

"I can't," I said. "The bars…the door is locked. I'm not going anywhere," I responded.

"Then let Him come in…"

And I saw Jesus walk into where I was. Suddenly there was a bench facing me on the other side of this small cell. Jesus sat and looked at me. I smiled, and then one of the ladies asked, "What is happening now?"

"He said He would just sit with me until I was ready to come out. We don't have to do anything. I don't have to move. He is just sitting," I said.

Then I noticed the bars were fading out of the picture and a garden was growing where the bars had just been. The garden was coming into my cell. Flowers were growing everywhere! Jesus and I just sat in the garden. "Thy Kingdom come," I said with understanding.

I laughed a little, and a prayer warrior asked, "What?"

"I'm not that big a fan of gardens…other people water flowers, not me."

"It must be beautiful," said both of the warriors.

KNOW WHERE YOU BELONG

My picture of sitting with Jesus in this garden gave me a deep sense of belonging, something with all my travels I rarely experience. Living overseas as long as I have, most of my life seems to be in adjusting to a new culture; and even when I head back to the United States, there is a period of learning how to fit in. I am always learning cultural norms that are not normal for me.

Several years ago I was arriving at Heathrow fairly early in the morning. The line heading into immigration wasn't long, but there were five men from Armenia ahead of me. These men were asked to step aside the queue and wait. The immigration man who had been gatekeeping, so to speak, also asked me to wait a minute while he dealt with them. He had to leave his post and pop out to get a specialist's assistance. The men from Armenia didn't look happy, but they sat on chairs and talked among themselves. They seemed nice enough people and many in the queue behind me expressed embarrassment on their behalf.

We were even more embarrassed when everyone at the head of the queue heard the police would be coming. These men were told, in front of everyone, that they would be heading back on the next plane. They were to be deported, even before they had legally entered the country. I must say that those of us who had lived in the United Kingdom for years, checked our own papers, hoping they were in order and that this deportation wasn't due to the bad mood of immigration that morning. I suppose that one of the most surprising aspects of this scene was that the immigration service had gone to the trouble to bring in someone who spoke Armenian, but wouldn't allow the men to speak. They were told in no uncertain terms that they would be leaving on the very next plane—or that is what I surmised by the hand gestures.

While I was reflecting on some of the teaching at Ellel, this memory of Heathrow airport came to mind. My flight into the United Kingdom reminded me that God sets the standard for whom and what gets into His Kingdom. To live in this place, you are required to be repentant; repentant of having lived anywhere else. You must express the desire of your heart to leave the ways of all other kingdoms behind and come into His. You express deep-as-you-can longing to learn His Kingdom ways. "My life," you say to the King of all kings, "is Yours." You don't even care to vacation to another land. You're finished traveling to places that have no life.

I knew, even without a stamped passport or certificate of church membership, that I was a member of this Kingdom of His. It wasn't that I needed "saving," to recover from having lived elsewhere. I was already saved. I didn't need to "get into His Kingdom." I was in it! I had been baptized by total immersion and later received the baptism of the Holy Spirit. In addition, I had been a member of a church for many, many years; but what really gave me the right to say I was His, was the fact He had said so! There is a Southern Gospel song that rings true to my mind when it says that the joy in your heart, knowing you are His, means one thing—not church membership or allegiance to religion—"you must have met Him."

Especially during this time out to wait and listen to the Holy Spirit, I have met with my Lord, and He has told me He loves me. And in this Kingdom and place He has prepared for me, I have come to know that He desires my recovery, for His name's sake. Recovery because I am, He says, a child of the King. No child of His sits around looking unloved. No child of His goes without knowing deep within that His hand is on his or her life. No child of His wanders around the world without purpose and a mapped-out plan. No child of His forgets how to worship with gusto. And every child of His knows how to dance.

With a song in my heart, just knowing I am His, I remember again and again the freedom key that enables me to wait on the Lord, watching the Master break the wall of hostility. Watching Him break this wall to say, "No child of Mine lives in a pit. No child of Mine gets walled in behind a wall of lies and bondage and entrapment. No child of Mine shall be kept from the life We have formed for them from the beginning of time." With a starting melody, I worship Him and say, "He forgives us as we forgive others," and I am so excited I just about dance as I say this over and over in the freedom of forgiveness. I am a prodigal who has come home; and I have made that decision of no turning back, no compromise with my life; and I understand that all aspects of life now come under His rule. *I got it* that I had lived a life of sin; I had lived my way. My way ended up in the pit, in a prison of sadness and loss of the life I was meant to live. This prodigal—me—has made a decision to live life God's way. No turning back. My identity is stamped forever. As it says in Ephesians 2:19 (NKJV) "Now, therefore, you are no more strangers and foreigners." I am accepted by the Beloved. I *am* accepted!

The Bible says it is Jesus who *broke down the middle wall of separation*,[4] the ceremonial law, often called *the partition wall*. It was referring to the partition in the temple that had every intent to separate the court of the Gentiles from the area where only the Jews had liberty to enter. They were His people. They were meant to tell us how to come into this freedom, and one rabbi rose and accepted that challenge. Jesus was telling me, "That hostility wall you are so worried about? That's *My* job to break it down!"

The wall of hostility is destroyed when we affirm, "Jesus is Lord."

> *For He Himself is our peace, who has made the two one and has destroyed the barrier, the dividing wall of hostility, by abolishing in His flesh the law with its commandments and regulations. His purpose was to create in Himself one new man out of the two, thus making peace. And in this one body to reconcile both of them to God through the cross, by which He put to death their hostility* (Ephesians 2:14-16).

ALONE IN MY ROOM

Alone on a sabbatical Saturday night, when on so many Saturday nights in the far country I sought a pleasure that did not exist outside His Kingdom, I began to know the deep pleasure of worshiping the King. I love to prepare my heart for Sunday morning worship, letting go of the week that is past and coming into His rest. Each Saturday that I keep this Shabbat preparation time, I am relieved of layer upon layer of the heaviness, the pinching pain on my shoulders of what I call "far country worry." A cool slip-stream of peace is injected into my spirit as I start to know that I can watch and wait as He guides me in stepping over the rubble of this hostile wall. He was and is breaking it down. I would not break down. If anything was going to break, it would be the wall.

I start to sing this anthem of a righteous land; in my Shabbat preparation time, I am learning words and marvelous things in a time and place meant for me. And the King whispers, "There's more...there is always more."

The Ezekiel Challenge for Today

The Ezekiel Challenge of the wall is met in Jesus. We see the anger of a righteous Father who could see a wall, a curtain, or anything that would separate us from His love and the way we were and are to live our lives. He promised in Ezekiel that He would tear down that wall! Tear it to pieces! He hated that divide. "When it [the wall] falls, you will be destroyed in it [he said to the prophets who whitewashed the divide]; and you will know that I am the Lord" (Ezek. 13:14). Once again we see that Jesus is the fulfilment of the prophesy from a true prophet, Ezekiel. Our challenge today is to see Jesus at every turn destroy the wall, take down the divide, and split the curtain in the temple that would keep us from approaching the Holy of Holies.

Personal Recovery Plan

The hostility wall exercise is one I like to do in my devotional time, and with small groups. The Holy Spirit taught me this exercise; when alone in our quiet time together, He brought it to my mind. This exercise allows us a way into understanding on a personal level that Jesus is the answer for breaking down walls of hostility between ourselves and members of our family. If we consider that a wall is often built brick by brick between ourselves and for example, our spouse, we can bring each brick in the wall before our Lord for Him to tear down. We need not spend wasted time whitewashing these bricks or the issues they represent, denying that the wall is there or that the cracks exist. We need not hide the wall.

You can start this exercise in your own quiet time by praying and asking the Holy Spirit to reveal to you someone in your family where there is a wall between you and that person. There may be several people who come to mind. Ask the Holy Spirit which person you should focus on at this time. Write the name of the person at the top of a piece of paper.

Under the name of the person you have selected, write numbers one to seven, or one to ten. You may have a hundred reasons why you cannot get along with this person, but start small and let the work of the Holy Spirit encourage you as you begin to see Him tear down the things that separate and resolve issues that create dissension. Spend some quiet time asking the Holy Spirit to label each brick in the wall.

For example, I recently did this exercise with regard to a family member I love, but we have struggled to connect and get along for any length of time. I know the Father wants us to live in harmony, but in the natural sense it didn't seem possible. We cannot change each other or make each other into someone we need them to be. Only God can change me and only God can change this relative of mine.

So, I wrote the person's name at the top of the page.

I prayed for this relative; praying that I would stop trying to play God in their lives (the eldest in a family can feel a little too responsible!), and for God to show me what I found challenging about the person. These challenges needed to not be from any soulish thinking on my part, but something that lined up with His Word. I needed to line up my will with His will for the person's life. I asked Father God to "label the bricks."

Brick number one became: language. I did not want to hear this person's foul language any more.

Brick two: intimidation. I did not want this person to use intimidation to get me to do what the person desired.

Brick three: boundaries. I want this person to respect my boundaries.

With each revelation, I wrote down the brick label and exactly the change I would like to see in the other person. I asked God what it was that *He* wanted for my relative. Then I compared the two. Did my desire for my relative line up with the Father's heart?

I even used some duplo bricks so that I could visualise the components of the wall that stood between us in our relationship. I made a choice to ask the Holy Spirit to speak to me about each brick. Did each brick label match a desire in *His heart* for this child of God?

I then prayed that I would no longer condemn this person for the bricks in this wall or try to change them. I prayed that the Holy Spirit would remove the bricks. Often I have been led to pray for one brick at a time and meditate on God's Word concerning these brick labels. I remind myself almost daily that it is not my job to tear down the wall, but the Lord's job! As I write this, God is revealing my own bricks that *stand in my relative's way of coming closer to me,* and most of the bricks in both our walls are disappearing. And something is being healed in our relationship.

Chapter 7

THE HIGH PASTURE

I will bring them out from the nations and gather them from the countries, and I will bring them into their own land, and I will pasture them on the mountains of Israel, in the ravines and in all the settlements in the land (Ezekiel 34:13).

So how do we do make this Ezekiel Challenge of recovery work?

Perhaps we could take a year or so off work and running a home to seek the Lord when it comes to recovering our family from brokenness, hurt, and damage. But no matter how much time we think we need to devote ourselves to family recovery, how do we find strength when we see our family fighting, not speaking, parting into separate rooms and towns, even broken beyond what we can repair? What happens if physical disease hits our loved ones and a family is divided in grief? How do we recover from the strain of health issues, disappointments, and the sadness of broken dreams for family life? If a family has experienced trauma from injury or an accident, how do we recover? And what about the effect of mental illness?

I've only listed a few of the many strains on family life today. There are addiction issues, including drugs and alcohol abuse, gambling, and pornography. There are financial issues, especially unemployment and debt. And what do we do with people who have wanted to control, dominate, or manipulate us—who have little concept of shared Christian values?

Most Christian living books focus on healthy, happy family life where we learn tips on how to get along. Some of us could be excused for being slightly overwhelmed with all that is set against our personal healthy, happy family life. When we read Christian articles on marriage or listen to a sermon on marriage and have a desperate hope to learn something, anything that would help, we could be excused for thinking that some people believe that most of us who ended up with a broken family *actually wanted* a divorce.

We could be excused—but not off the hook. *What if God* wants you to step up and accept an impossible assignment to work to restore your family—and I mean every member of your family, not just a select and favored few? What if He is calling you to the ultimate challenge of your life, to not give up on your husband who battles bi-polar issues, alcoholism, or diabetes—or give up on your wife with anorexia, your rebellious child? Please, I beg you to not put this book down before at least considering that your current challenge could have a happy ending.

I had to face this challenge. God had a dream for my family. I had a dream for my family. The two dreams did not match.

A Mission Assignment

In Chapter 6, The Wall of Hostility, we looked at the fact that when we choose to forgive others who have hurt us, or forgive ourselves for what we have done or not done, often it is still an impossible challenge to establish reconciliation or begin the process of restoring our lives. Especially when you are dealing with a tough assignment. None of us are the "Brady Bunch."[1]

I'm not talking about the need to tidy up the living room so we feel comfortable watching television on Saturday night. Wouldn't it be wonderful if restoring marriages was that easy? And yet, that is how broken families are often treated when we cry for help.

We get a message that broken hearts and broken homes are all a matter of tidying up a few things and all will be well. What do you do when you have forgiven everything and everyone and done everything you know to do and still things fall apart?

For those of us who see separation from our spouse as our only choice, it is because we have hit a wall of hostility at every turn. The wall of hostility, as noted in Ephesians 2, is standing in the way of overcoming all that would keep us from a restored life. As difficult as it may sound, if we don't whitewash the wall, or walls, and pretend to be happy families when we are anything but, then maybe this wall can be what stops us in our tracks and helps us look for the serious help we need.

Facing this wall may give us hope. When a brick or two have challenging labels beyond our skill set, we need to call on divine intervention. We need to cry out for help. We don't pretend we can do this mission. *We know* we can only step over the rubble of a torn down wall *when we see* that Father God has, indeed, torn down the wall.

But let me remind you that this mission message is for Christians. It is for people who have called on His name and know that they desire to be His people. If you have not given your life to Jesus, and yet you are serious about recovering from all that is broken in you and in your family, then ask Him into your heart. No matter how crushed your spirit or how broken your heart, no matter how chaotic your situation, if you ask Jesus to come into your mind, will, and emotions, you begin to make Him Lord of your whole life, and that includes recovery of your spirit, soul, and body. That includes the whole family![2]

Second, *recognize* that we are made of spirit, soul, and body, and ask His Holy Spirit to bring new life to your spirit. Many, many Christians say we receive the Holy Spirit when we accept Jesus into our life. I believe that is true, but often things we receive need activation. The Holy Spirit told the believers to go to the upper room and wait. They were believers all, but they needed to *wait for the power* to come on them. The Holy Spirit needed to bring their spirit alive with His power!

I had to spend time, quiet time, trusting the Father to awaken my spirit to hear all He wanted to say to me. I had to tell Him I wanted to know His still, small voice, and I wanted to *know* that voice without a doubt. This brought me to a place where I felt safe to be obedient to all He told me to do.[3]

Third, even if no pastor or church leader finds you and leads you to a place that restores you and your family, know that Father God will do it. He will find you! He found me in my own living room. There I was, in a relationship where it was more trouble than it was worth for me to attend a mid-week women's ministry meeting where I could learn how to be the godly wife I always longed to be—so I found Joyce Meyer on the television. I couldn't attend church teaching, so Father God started right where I was with His plan for my life by bringing teaching into my home! For the first time in my life, I heard someone preach who hadn't had a perfect life and who knew how to reach out to say to others, "You too can come into this freedom."

It would seem like light years from the time I first heard this freedom teaching and the time I would walk in freedom myself; but step by small step, He showed me He has a plan for healing and recovery from every situation, and it's a good plan (see Jer. 29:11).

If you join me in taking on this mission for yourself and for your family,[4] be prepared to be amazed. Be prepared to see that His plan is detailed and written just for you—your own Personal Recovery Plan. It's *how you* become an overcomer.[5] This plan will guide you to trust Him as He tears down, brick by brick if He has to, the wall of hostility facing you. As you see this wall turn to rubble, He will show you how to step over the rubble to step into a place of restoration.

As you gain understanding of the Father's heart for your recovery from addiction, illness, abuse, bereavement, or emotional breakdown, you will see that while there are some similarities for anyone in recovery, the Father actually has a plan that is just for you! He promises that He "will seek that which was lost, and bring again that which was driven away, and will bind up that which was broken, and will strengthen that which was sick!" (Ezek. 34:16 KJV). He is serious about you!

If you are one of His sheep, He *wants* you to hear His voice. How would you be able to follow Him if you can't hear Him? Spiritual abuse comes in strong when you can hear others, but cannot hear His voice for yourself. You need *His* voice to confirm that what you read (and I mean this book or any other) is for *you* at any particular time.

You need *His* voice when others tell you what to do. You need to hear *His* voice to confirm that He is using an elder or someone in authority to guide you. All advice needs to line up with Scripture and be confirmed by the voice of the Father that you are coming to know and love. As you read this book, test what you read. Ask the Father, "Is this for me? Are You speaking to me through these words at this time?"

Hearing His voice also keeps you from wasting your time. If you haven't noticed, magazines and pop psychology speak to your soul. Your soul is your mind, will, and emotions, and they are a big money market. Anytime you let your soul be in charge of what you do, your emotions reign, and you are not setting yourself up for healing success. Tell your soul to be still—your spirit is listening to the Holy Spirit!

Your Father is speaking through the Holy Spirit to your spirit to lead you to a place of recovery. We will talk more about the role of the church, and His pastoral shepherds, in the last part of this book; but for now, know that in the name of Jesus the Father will guide you. When you hear His voice, you can trust Him. For those of us who have been victims of abuse or trauma, whether in childhood or later years, it is the ultimate challenge to trust. This is no small challenge. You, like me, have to know the voice of the Shepherd to trust each and every step in any journey of restoration. It is my testimony that He will lead you to step over the wall of hostility and step over what becomes rubble as He tears it down—it is safe to step into His healing place.

It's called the high pasture.

The High Pasture

The high pasture is a sheep pen for recovery of lost, broken, and sick sheep. It is a "good place,"[6] and that means a place where you can trust what you hear. You are safe[7] and you know in your knower that the Shepherd's plans are for your good and not for evil (see Jer. 29:11). Your "blind side"[8] is covered. You do not have to watch your back in this place. What happens here *is* for your good.

This pasture is a "high place"[9] where you can gain a perspective and take time to see where you have been and consider where you are going in life. The mountain heights of Israel were considered the best place to be, and your personal high pasture will be the best place for your healing. People build forts on high places so they can be ready for the enemy and they are protected. This high pasture of yours is a protected place.

This pasture is a "fat place."[10] This is the King James word for the fact that what the Lord provides is not lean or mean. There will be plenty for you to graze on, and you do not even have to think about your recovery plan on a tight budget. All you need will be provided; or as is said in the New International Version, "There they will lie down [ah, rest!] in good grazing land, and there they will feed in a rich pasture..." (Ezek. 34:14)

How Do I Get There?

You do not come into this pen, this place of beautiful restoration, unless you are beckoned by the Shepherd. That Shepherd is Jesus Christ, the Son of the Lord God Almighty. Make no mistake about it, many, many people have tried throughout the ages to get to this healing place via other shepherds, gods, gurus, and philosophies, but there is no security system like the boundaries of this pasture. You only get in via *the* Shepherd. Listening to other voices will get you to a place of deception where, for a time, you will think you are in recovery and you think you will have had a cool drink of refreshing water—but you will be thirsty again.

"It didn't work," they say of the latest rehab.

"While I thought it was good, that counseling only made my situation worse," you hear time and again.[11]

"The medicine was almost as bad as the illness."

And one of the worst results of this faux recovery path, I believe in God's eyes, is that some are acting as in the time of Ezekiel, when many used the name of religion to sell someone a blessing.[12] There are so-called evangelists and faith healers who only want to fill the church to feed their own stomachs and do not care about the sheep. They do not care for you, your family, your restoration, or your recovery from sickness and brokenness; they do not care when you have become lost and prey to the wolves. They only care for their bottom line.

These are as the days of Ezekiel. I believe we need to hear the message of Ezekiel again, in this time. We need to hear Father God's response to times like these. He says, "Woe to the shepherds of Israel [His people]!" If they do not take their responsibilities before Him seriously, He has sent Jesus! He sent Him once, and He will come again. In the meantime, Jesus lives in us through the life of the Holy Spirit, and the Holy Spirit is more than capable to guide us to the Father's place of recovery.

Ezekiel told us about this type of recovery. He warned us that the Lord God was serious about shepherds and His people who have been healed; we have a responsibility to share the high pasture message. He warned us that we need to care for the sheep of His pasture, and He would send a Shepherd to show us just how to do this. This prophesy came true, and we have a living Lord who is just as serious about recovery today.

If we are His, He will guide us and show us the way to the high pasture. No other name knows the way—or the truth and the life He wants for us, for that matter.

So, you get to the high pasture by listening to the Holy Spirit. When you know His voice, you can trust Him to guide you to where He "will look after" you.

For this is what the Sovereign Lord says: I Myself will search for My sheep and look after them. As a shepherd looks after his scattered flock when he is with them, so will I look after My sheep. I will rescue them from all the places where they were scattered on a day of clouds and darkness. I will bring them out from the nations and gather them from the countries, and I will bring them into their own land, I will pasture them on the mountains of Israel, in the ravines and in all the settlements in the land (Ezekiel 34:11-13).

What will we find when we get there?

Ezekiel 34:13 says that God "will bring them out from the nations and gather them from the countries, and I will bring them to their own land."

First of all, it will be for you. Just you. You will know in your "knower"[13] as you wait upon the Lord and begin to truly listen to what He has to say to you, that what He is saying *is for you*. You want to own the land, own the recovery place, and know that it is for you and no one else. He says you will have your own land, your own place in the pasture. It lines up with His Word, and you will know in your spirit (not necessarily your mind, will, or emotions) that the Holy Spirit is claiming territory for your healing.

I Will Pasture Them on the Mountains of Israel. . .

Second, there will be mountains in this good pasture of yours. In other words, there will be issues that arise that only He can settle. Just as you needed to stand back and see and hear how He was and is tearing down the wall of hostility between you and all that would keep you from the life He has for you, there will be mountains only He can move. Many a Sunday I have been glad the worship team has led us to sing, "He can move the mountains! My God is mighty to save!"[14] There has been more than one mountain in my good pasture.

Mountains can also be tests we need to pass so that we can heal or come into freedom in some area of our lives. As Joyce Meyer says, "I might as well pass my test. I do not want to go around this mountain one more time!"[15] It is in the good pasture that you get it, you understand that sometimes these mountains are just tests we need to pass, and He has provided them just for you, to show you where you are strong, and that He is strong to deliver.[16]

And then there is the mountain top. It's the place where the Lord is high and lifted up. It is where the serious issues meet with the perspective of God. You can reread the stories of Moses and listen again to sermons about the mountain top experiences that show you how to live; however, I believe there is a fresh word given even in these times.

Dr. Martin Luther King Jr. spoke of his mountain top experience.[17] It showed the vision of the journey ahead. You hear God up there, and you are never the same. You cannot live up there, but when you come back for rest by the still waters, you are changed forever.

Above all, the mountains of Israel were the *best places*, the protected place, and He wants the best, protected place for your recovery.

...In the Ravines

When He brings us into the ravines, our Savior is bringing us into a deep, narrow valley[18] or gorge worn by running water, even a stream. Originally, ravine is a late 18th century word meaning violent rush of water.[19] But an interesting feature of a ravine being part of the high pasture is that a stream that forges the ravine is crucial to the water cycle. And the most exciting aspect of this feature is that the biological habitation in the immediate vicinity of a stream is called a riparian zone! This is the zone, *created from the beginning of time*, that our Father set up for the role of connecting fragmented habitats. This high pasture is a repair zone!

All over the world, the importance of these zones has led to a surge of restoration activities aimed at getting these zones back in shape.[20] We need them. Our earth was created with these zones; and what we see in the physical world, we see our Father has set up for us in the high pasture of our own recovery. He knew what He was saying when He said that in the high pasture He would bring us to "the ravines."

In the high pasture we find that He has everything ready for our recovery and repair. I mentioned that streams play an important role in connecting fragmented habitats. If you take this analogy and apply it to your emotional world, is your life fragmented[21] beyond human restoration? Is your heart broken into a thousand pieces that you cannot glue back yourself?

We often say we are "shattered," when we are tired beyond belief and cannot sort out the mess or win the battle to get our kids healed, or our lives glued back together—and we are right. We cannot do this on our own. For some of us, if we took a bottle and smashed it on the sidewalk, the result would display the splintered mess of our lives, and we cannot glue the pieces back together. We cannot make our world whole again or even put the bottle back together in some useful fashion. But we have the King of kings who can; and it is in the high pasture that He says He intends to restore us to the life He designed for us from the beginning.

...And in All the Settlements in the Land

Fourth, there are the settlements. This is where we learn to live again with others. We learn how to be part of the community in the Kingdom of God. We learn our role in the community. We stop trying to be someone we are not. We ask the Father "Who am I? Who did You make me to be? What are my gifts and talents?" In the high pasture we learn to be real about the work we do in the Kingdom.

It is in the high pasture that we come to an understanding of Kingdom living and its principles.

Starting the Journey to the High Pasture

My "year out," to seek the Lord was well under way, but I was panicking a little, as it seemed I had taken a good part of the year to learn that there even was a high pasture. I wanted to spend another year just *being in* the high pasture! It more worried me that I still needed to figure out how to get to this high healing place.

One day I was on a walk—as the Holy Spirit had walks feature highly in my personal plan—asking myself questions as I was walking. I decided to spend a little time praying and asked God, "*If* You were to heal, how would You heal me? By what means?" Nothing too holy, no pious words. Just a question directed to God.

Immediately, I heard the audible voice *that I knew* was my Shepherd! "Music," He said. That was all. Just the word music. I was surprised, as my sister was known as the musical one, not me. Still, if He said it, it must be what He meant to say. I made a mental note to start listening to music, maybe some worship music, or something on the radio. I wasn't sure. And then I kept walking and thinking and praying—wondering what He meant, and even more curious as to what God could or would do with me through music.

It was early in the morning when I returned to Pierrepont, a campus of Ellel Ministries International, and I decided to go into the student lounge for some quiet time. I was a student in the Never Ever The Same (NETS) course,[22] taking time to study and search the Father's heart for my life. Actually, it was my broken heart, shattered beyond human repair, that I wanted Him to mend. I knew He was up to something this morning.

Being England in the summer, the morning was damp; but there was a light to it that all artists love. The light came through the trees and the grass was fresh and green. As I walked the path to the student common rooms, I realized I was noticing trees again. Long ago I had a love for the forest. When did I lose that? When did fear of a walk in the woods become greater than my need for being among the tall trees? I brushed off these thoughts and went into the building.

Often there was an early riser already at prayer in these rooms, but I found one that was empty. As I went in and closed the door, I heard again the audible voice that I know to be my Shepherd. "See the piano?"

"Yes, Lord."

"Well, take a seat."

"At the piano?"

"Yes."

I sat on the stool and looked at the keyboard. "OK, Lord. I'm sitting…what are we doing here?"

The whole place was early-morning quiet. Light filtered in from the windows, and I just sat still. I prepared my heart for what He was about to say.

"This is where it began," He said.

"What began?"

"Your rebellion. This is where your rebellion began...and you were six years old." I knew exactly what He meant. My mother had tried to get me to study and practice the piano, and I had been determined to rebel against anything that she asked me to do, especially piano practice. This is where a determined and rebellious spirit had entered my spirit.

"This is where the rebellion started," I heard the Father say again. "Right here on a piano stool. You wanted to reject her so badly that you even rejected the very way she could connect with you."

Waves of emotion in wanting to run away from her came to the surface of my mind. Even now I could almost slam the piano! "God! What she did..." But I couldn't go that route with God. Suddenly I felt so sorry, so deeply sorry as I could see that I hurt my mother and that this had been my way of rejecting *anything* she wanted to give me. If she wanted to give me the gift of learning music, I wanted nothing to do with it.

Then He melted a slice of my heart.

"Can't you see that she loved you? And it was through music she was trying to reach you?" He asked.

I had built up so much of my life based on a lie I believed, of not being loved but of being rejected from birth, that I didn't know what to do with a concept that my mother might have loved me. *Strange kind of love,* I thought; but I caught a glimpse of that love and knew that I had slammed the door shut. So many people had said to me over the years that my kind and loving mother was a "second mother" to them; I wanted a first mother! Bewildered and full of regret, in an instant I could see what I had done to her, and I wept. Tears flowed and flowed silently. I buried my head in my hands.

"Dear God, I am so sorry."

In a minute or two, I sat up and wiped my face. "OK, Lord. We are still sitting here." In no sense did He release me to move from the piano stool. I continued to sit, knowing He wanted me to practice being still and knowing that He is God—not moving until I felt His release.

I sat looking at the keys, picturing all the piano books my mother had placed before me. I remembered the lies my mother told my piano teacher when she finally realized I had transferred my hatred to this lovely friend of hers who had as a favor agreed to teach me. Pictures came of the ball of hatred growing in me, anger that resulted in a thirteen-year-old running away on the streets of the city. And then running away again at sixteen.

"Dear God, I am sorry," and I knew He knew I was sorry.

I looked again at the keyboard. "I don't know what to do with this. It's too late."

Just then the door of the student lounge opened slightly. Merlyn, another NETS student, popped her head in. She smiled at me, and I felt slightly embarrassed. Here was a worship leader who leads hundreds if not thousands with her music at her and her husband's church in India, and I was sitting at the piano.

"What are you doing?" she had that lovely smile again.

"I don't know. I don't know what I am doing here." I said.

"Would you like to learn to play?"

I thought a moment, tempted to lie but truth came. "Yes. Yes, I would."

Merlyn quietly closed the door behind her and walked over to me.

"But it's too late." I said.

"Oh no, it's not. Would you like me to show you a secret that we do in India? I will share it with you, if you would like me to. We can have you playing quickly. It's what we have to do back home when we need people to lead worship and haven't had time or money for lessons. It is what I did."

I couldn't believe it. Merlyn had the most beautiful voice, and she played in a way that made people stop whatever they were doing to listen. She had a huge church to lead in India and a national ministry to start, but here she was teaching me. I learned two chords that day. There would be more. Each time I needed to learn a new chord; for God gave me a song, Merlyn would amazingly show up on these mornings and say, "The next chord is…" and show me. Little by little, the song came together, and He said I was to follow the music to the high pasture, that place He had prepared for me on earth as it is in Heaven.

Chapter 8

LISTENING AND BOUNDARIES

I will search for the lost and bring back the strays. I will bind up the injured and strengthen the weak, but the sleek and the strong I will destroy. I will shepherd the flock with justice (Ezekiel 34:16).

Years ago when I was a young teenager, my father woke up me, my sister, and my brother quite early one morning. Mother had prepared a picnic, and Dad was piling us into the car. I could feel Dad's excitement for the day ahead. He was going to show us something he said "we would never forget."

We headed from the suburbs of Arlington, Virginia, to downtown Washington, DC. We took this route every Sunday as our church was on Sixteenth Street, but today we were stopping by a park area that I had mostly known as a site for football games or families picnicking. It was difficult to find a parking place, but eventually we were out of the car and traipsing around a temporary community being set up for a weekend of Washington protests. They called this campsite, Resurrection City.

My father was a quiet, Southern Baptist with a slightly reserved bent, so I hope you'll understand that to see him so excited made us all curious to say the least. He was a lawyer so he could see history in everything, but on this day he said it was "an historic day."

All we could see was a mass of people putting up tents and hammering in tent pegs. I did notice that *all* the people were black but my pale, Scottish heritage father never ever seemed to notice race, so it didn't surprise me when he led the way among the tents and kept pointing out things. "Look at this, it is so exciting!" he said, and then, "Look, over there, I think that's him!"

"Who, Dad?"

"Reverend, Doctor Martin Luther King. He's a Baptist, you know." Dad was very proud of fellow Baptists and this Baptist especially. He made us stand very still as we watched some important looking men pound tent pegs. Photographers were everywhere. Whether it was Dr. King or not, bent over in a suit and pounding a peg for the front page of some newspaper, I will never know, but it was always being drummed into us in subtle and not so subtle ways the humble actions of truly great men.

Dad told us that Dr. King would be speaking later and that we would stay to hear him. Now I was really excited, as Dad was head of one of the divisions of the Justice Department and that usually meant we would have up-front seats. I had heard from both my parents about the Civil Rights moment, and remembered the times I had seen my mom and dad weeping over tragedies—over six little girls who died in Sunday school when a bomb had hit their place of worship. I would hear my parent's dinner conversation, anger over "negros not being allowed to vote." Now, it was amazing to me that we would have the opportunity to hear this great man speak.

In the meantime that morning, Dad took us to stand on the street corner. Now we were watching buses. Loads of yellow school buses pulling into the city. Arms were waving out of windows and people were singing freedom songs. Dad said they were "freedom riders," and had come from places like Alabama and Mississippi, states my deeply Southern family knew well.

"Is Arkansas coming?" my younger siblings asked. That was Dad's home state.

"I hope we see Arkansas here, look for the licence plates," he said. We spent ages playing that old road trip game, and each time we saw a new state plate we would call it out to Dad. He just laughed and said, "Good. That's good. Keep them coming."

We had our picnic and talked about all the buses we had seen and where they were from. Neither Mom or Dad were much interested in the Northern plates, but each time we mentioned "I saw one from Georgia," or "that place near Grandma's in Charlotte," they would look at each other and just beam.

Mom told us we would be heading to the Lincoln Memorial for the speech, and that it reminded her of the time she and Dad had attended a concert at Constitution Hall. Apparently Marian Anderson, a black American opera singer, was giving a concert; but at the start of the performance, Mrs. Anderson was asked to leave. There was some announcement about "colored people" not singing at Constitution Hall. Mrs. Anderson walked out with dignity, my mother remembered— and then everyone followed this gracious lady all the way to the steps of the Lincoln Memorial.

To this day, my mother is convinced this is the reason Dr. King gave his speech on the same spot. To her, it wasn't just the history of Lincoln.

I don't remember the hour we left our picnic and headed for the Memorial, but I do remember it was daylight, and I was looking to get us a good place to sit and hear the great man speak. Dad had my brother on his shoulders, and my sister held my mother's hand. I was running ahead of my family and working to get us right up front.

My dad called to me, "We won't be up there today."

"Why not? Don't you have the reservation? Don't they know who you are?" We were proud of our dad working in the Justice Department, meeting with Robert Kennedy every week and the President of the United States every month. Dad was head of the Land Division, but he would also bring home ideas such as the Peace Corps from his boss and he was passionate about the work of civil rights that was developing in the Division of Justice headed by one of his colleagues. Surely we would get to get up close and hear this famous speaker today.

At that time I was only moments away from hearing about a dream, a vision of land promised where children of all colors could play together. We were only an hour or two away from hearing the description of a dream that would inspire us to a new reality of righteousness, boundary lines drawn in justice and a godly freedom. We needed, we *wanted* to hear every word; and to my young thinking, I needed to be up next to this man. Surely we should be there, somewhere in the front rows.

But Dad placed a restraining hand, "No. Not today. There are some people who deserve to be in the front rows for this speech, and we aren't the ones."

LISTENING FOR THE NEW BOUNDARIES

If ever someone knew how to set new boundaries for a land promised by God, it was Dr. King. Adjusted boundaries and adjusted thinking would be the requirements for the day as we adjusted how we lived along Kingdom lines. We needed to hear the vision and know it was from God.

When we are so deep in the pit, we don't know what freedom looks like; when we are so behind the bars of a prison cell of bondage to ungodly brokenness and demonic imaginations, we need to hear from the Holy Spirit what it looks like "out there." The only way out is Him coming in, giving us His living Word describing a new neighborhood.

Dr. King described God's dream, requiring new boundaries for His Kingdom living here on earth, as it was in Heaven. Not everyone gets a dream like this, a mountaintop experience or even a clear picture from the Lord; but we need to hear the description words. We need to hear words that tell us God has a dream *for us*—words from a dreamer that describe for us, inspire us to believe we can rest in Father God's recovery place as a people under the authority of God, indivisible, with liberty and justice. Dr. King always made it clear he had read the Scriptures, and what he was sharing was to the best of his knowledge from a God of hope. There was hope for God's dream in America.

Hope refined is a timely word that encourages, "you can do it." You don't have to live any other way than the way God intends for you to live. You *can* recover from the bondage of bigotry, from destructive communication and pride. You *can* leave drugs behind in another world. Gambling *can* be a distant memory. Alcohol? Homosexuality?

Verbal abuse? Bruises and the night terror for you and your children? You can overcome.

Dr. King described a dream[1] of new boundaries for the way we would live if we were to recover the land from the brokenness of bigotry. These boundaries would help us recover from the time of slavery, both mental and physical. In this new thinking, we could begin to walk in a freedom we had never known, where even the children would reap a godly legacy.

YOUR FIRST ATTEMPTS AT BOUNDARIES

I still recall the great feeling I had when I attended my first teaching on boundaries. I, like others, held my head a little more confidently as we walked out of the church hall that day. Why had it never dawned on us? Of course, set a boundary! It was even more encouraging to read the books coming out on boundaries; and to this day, I believe those books are an essential part of recovery.[2] Yet, these first attempts at setting a boundary often ended in failure.

As part of my recovery sabbatical, I wanted to take time to have a serious look at boundaries, my boundaries. Why had I never been successful at setting boundaries? Why couldn't I create a safe place for recovery? I wasn't talking about changing the world, but simply starting with me—my safe place for recovering from a broken heart and returning to a life of freedom.

In one of our story-sharing times, my friend Rachel told me about her first attempts at boundary setting. She told how she set a boundary with her telephone. "I asked my ex-spouse not to call me or text me…he was, after all, married again. I set this boundary as I needed a time of recovery including good conversations with people, not being drawn in by someone who led me to make unhealthy choices. But still he would send a text and ask me to meet up with him for lunch. I felt defeated. I told him my boundary again…my phone was off limits to him. For a couple of months he respected my request, but then he called again. Oh, he apologized for disregarding my desire, but he kept on contacting me."

Rachel, like many people who wish to establish firm boundaries, found that time and time again people ignore what is said and do what they want to do. She tried to establish a new rule for herself, one that she believed was according to the new life Jesus has designed for her. Unfortunately, she found herself almost bulldozed down by not just her ex-husband, but by friends and family running roughshod over her feeble attempts at boundary setting. Her recovery place didn't seem much like the high pasture promised in Ezekiel. Rachel knew that to get to that high pasture and stay there until she was healed of the hurts and the damage of the past, she was going to have to build a strong boundary around all that she did in her life. If God was going to have the time and space to work on healing her broken heart, she needed that safe protected place so she could meet with the Father.

"But what do I do? No one seems to be listening!" she asked. We were both on a mission to find out.

Preparation for Boundary Building

Many people enjoy painting, decorating, and gardening, but not many enjoy the prep work. It's not that we can't paint a wall in a day, we can; but if we hurry the preparation stage, we know we will be re-painting again all too soon.

Rachel and I discovered it's the same with setting boundaries for godly recovery. We knew it is *His* high pasture where the Lord has provided all we need (see Ezek. 34:14). From the Bible, we knew it is a safe place if we stay in the boundaries of how He intends for us to live while we are in recovery; but we also knew boundaries aren't easy to establish.

We learned that we needed to allow for preparation time for boundary building.

Nehemiah

Many liken setting boundaries to building a wall. Nehemiah was the great wall builder in the Old Testament.[3] He looked at the materials he needed, he enlisted others to help, and he organized himself for dealing with the detractors. He set guards ready to defend; establishing protection from those who would not simply run over the new wall, but tear it down.

We needed to do something similar, accepting that people were not going to be excited for us when we set out a new boundary.

Dr. King also talks about the need for preparation when setting a new course in his Letter from Birmingham Jail,[4] "Privileged groups seldom give up their privileges voluntarily." Make note of who has privileges when you are without boundaries.

He goes on to say that, "In any non-violent campaign" (I presume you are committed to nonviolence in your life and in your home. Let's not shoot the ones we are called to love!) "there are four basic steps:

1. Collection of the facts to determine whether injustice exists

2. Negotiation

3. Self-purification

4. Direct action."[5]

If you look at Rachel's situation, trying to put a boundary between her and her old life, you see the injustice of a marriage to someone who has no intention of being faithful—not even now that he is married to someone else. She has the facts of infidelity.

If you are coming out of a life of drugs or gambling addiction, you will have enough facts to last you a lifetime. The life you have led is not for your good. A life of alcoholism or anorexia is no life at all. You already have the facts!

You can then look at point number 2: Negotiation. With whom have you negotiated? When Dr. King was struggling to lead Americans out of the bondage of a slavery mentality, to recover a people from a second class citizen existence, he noted great resistance with everyone whom he had tried to negotiate. "As in so many past experiences, our hopes had been blasted, and the shadow of deep disappointment settled upon us."[6] It wasn't working!

It takes two or two sides to negotiate. It takes a respectful conversation where both parties are listening, really listening, to have a successful negotiation. Whether this is a history-making negotiation or simply one that changes your personal life, the other person(s) needs to be listening for you to be able to negotiate boundaries.

We can't just decide we are going to have a boundary, no matter how good the intent, and expect all concerned to go, "Oh, OK. Sure, I see your point." It is not, in most cases, going to happen. We need to prepare ourselves for setting boundaries sometimes without the approval of others who stand to lose by you being whole and wholly a child of God; and that brings us to Dr. King's third point.

PURIFICATION

From the Birmingham prison, Dr. King wrote that, "We decided to undertake a process of self-purification. We began a series of workshops on non-violence, and we repeatedly asked ourselves; 'are you able to accept the blows without retaliating? Are you able to endure the ordeal of jail?'"[7]

You may never be called to go to jail. You may never be called to stand in streets under the blow of fire hoses, but you will have consequences for your boundaries. A boundary isn't a boundary just by decree; it stands as a boundary when you can take the consequences. Rachel had to not only set her boundary, "He will not call me," she then had to block his number. She had to withstand the emotional challenge of not answering his calls. A child of a friend of mine, working to come into the freedom of a drug free life, left rehab saying, "I have a boundary around my new friendship group. No drug pusher is a friend," and then he moved out of the neighborhood.

A major part of preparing ourselves for successful boundary setting is in answering Dr. King's question: Are you able to endure the ordeal of _____ and fill in the blank. In your quiet time, ask Father God to prepare you for handling consequences, seen and unseen, as you set new boundaries for living a life recovered, restored, and forgiven.

Prepare for Tension

We are in deception if we mislead ourselves into thinking we can just announce our new boundaries and people will fall over themselves to comply. Are you kidding? Just tell that to a newly diagnosed cancer patient. Just tell that to someone who has been betrayed at work and can't find a new job. Just tell that to someone who has just left the court house with fresh divorce papers they never wanted. Just tell that to a child of a sex offender.

We may or may not be setting the course of history but these are difficult times, and we are handling challenging issues; for as Christians, we have full intention to live the life Jesus died to give us. Again, Dr. King from the Birmingham jail, "...I must confess I am not afraid of the word 'tension.' I have earnestly opposed violent tension, but there is a type of constructive, nonviolent tension which is necessary for growth."[8]

Are you ready for the tension that comes when you set boundaries? Let's start by knowing how some of the best boundaries are made.

Your Boundary: Stone Wall or Fortress?

I had come a long way in my sabbatical year. I met the challenge of recognizing any self-pity deep within me and came into the reality of needing to get angry. I have recovered a righteous anger and have started to practice spiritual warfare, understanding that the battle is between spiritual municipalities and not among humankind. I have started practicing being angry at the right things; and at the cross I have aimed at gaining the understanding that forgiveness is not in and of itself reconciliation or restoration. I know that the Word of God has said that forgiveness opens the door to reconciliation and restoration; but often as forgiveness becomes a reality, I see that a wall of hostility emerges. I have tried to handle that wall myself, and then came to understand that the tearing down of this wall is the Lord's work. He is the One to reconcile all things to Himself.[9]

The Father has brought me to a good place; that place where I am restored in His high pasture for all that has gone on when I was in the far country. In that restoration, I do see a new way of living. I am choosing to live according to His Kingdom. To protect that way of life that has been promised to me and to all who have come into the freedom of His forgiveness, I took confidence in setting some boundaries.

"Which boundaries, Lord?" I had learned to not set boundaries of my own imagination, but ones that were from Him to me. Not my mother, not my father, not my sister, not my brother, but me.

"Keep the Sabbath," He said.

"Yes, I know Lord. That's in Your commandments. The *Old* Ten Commandments," I said.

"I know how old they are," He replied, "and what I want other people to do, but you are to be in church on Sundays. That's My gift to you."

So it may not surprise you, though it did surprise me at the time, that on the very next Sunday I really struggled with getting myself up and going—and that the sermon turned out to be on which subject?

Boundaries.

We are privileged to have Dr. Russ Parker as part of our church. Actually, we are privileged to have every member of our wild little fellowship, but Dr. Parker, Russ, happens to be Director of the Acorn Christian Healing Center (Christian Listeners, in America) and travels worldwide teaching on healing wounded history. He happened to be home and preaching on this particular Sunday.

In his sermon, he shared that "in our brokenness and hurt we often build a boundary that is a wall around us that doesn't work; and one of the reasons it doesn't work, is that there are no doors or windows in our wall."

We may think we have set a boundary as a wall of protection, but it is not God's healing place "if poison is trapped inside." We need doors to let out the poison in our hearts and minds, and doors to let in God's love. We need windows to let out the poison of hatred and bitterness, and an open window to what the Holy Spirit wants to do if we allow Him in.[10]

If we see our boundary as a fortress, we see a strong tower built on a high place. It is a good safe place, but again it needs doors and windows, even a drawbridge. A fortress is a more imposing picture than a simple wall, but it is an excellent metaphor for setting boundaries that hold in the more challenging battles.

So with preparation for setting a boundary, including accepting the role of hard work and tension in this endeavor, I was almost ready to begin again with boundary setting.

But, there was still something bothering me.

In the course of my search and in the excitement of learning about the Father's healing high pasture, many people had asked, "Why do you think terrible things happen to so many families in the first place?"

I needed to look at this issue if I was to understand the doors and windows within my boundary wall.

Chapter 9

WHY?

So they were scattered because there was no shepherd, and when they were scattered they became food for all the wild animals (Ezekiel 34:5).

OVER THE WHOLE EARTH

Elizabeth was raised in a small village in northern Germany where her father was the Burgermeister, or mayor. Elizabeth was my mother-in-law, and she told me this story on a grey afternoon in England. Though it was light years past the events of the time, sadness was deep in her voice.

"At first," she said of her father, "he really liked Hitler. We all did, for the way he encouraged the youth and improved many things. Father had no problem with implementing the directives that came down from the party. We had a picture of the Furher in our home. Then things changed. It became more and more difficult for Father to carry out the orders given to Burgermeisters throughout our area."

Elizabeth smiled briefly when she remembered, "Some days my mother turned the picture of Hitler over to face the wall; and on some days when it might be noticed, she turned it back around. My father was not a hero. He wanted to do what was right, and he struggled with the new commands. Still, he could not stand up to those over him, and his blood pressure rose. He would say a little, to someone in the government about his opinion on the new commands, not just for the Jews, but other things. It was a very stressful time; but instead of outright protest, he had a heart attack and he died."

"And?" I said gently to my mother-in-law, for she was telling me all this after I had asked her about her brother.

"Well, it seems that by that time, they [I'm not sure who "they" were] knew my father's politics and his views on things against the Nazi party, so they sent my brother to the Russian steps. We never saw him again. Mother died not knowing what happened to my brother. That's what happened to anyone who did not agree with the government."

One side of the Red Cross that I dearly love is the work they do to search for people lost in battle or natural disaster; and one day a letter came. It had the heading of the International Red Cross, and in the letter which Elizabeth showed me it said they had found Herr Pillenkamp, her brother. He was buried in a mass grave in Kiev.

"Would you like to go?" I asked Elizabeth, offering to go with her.

"Not now, I am not sure about seeing the grave, but at least we know."

THE BROKEN

Dr. Russ Parker, Director of Acorn Christian Healing Center (Christian Listeners Association) tells of a woman in Burundi, a country in Central Africa. Joy (not her real name), received one of his team into her living space at a refugee camp. The woman had a terrible story to tell and tears rolled down her face as she spoke of the beatings and the rape she had experienced—and the carnage she had witnessed. Her family had been destroyed.

"But what amazed me about Jesus," she said, "is that He would send you to listen to me. He must love me." It healed something in her that our Lord would send someone in the flesh just to listen.[1]

Pastor Charles Rowley teaches Celebrate Recovery in the United States. He's from Kansas, but on a visit to the Vietnam Memorial in Washington, DC, he noticed that, "A lot of veterans hang out around that wall." He looked at the wall and eventually sat down next to a vet. "The vet started talking, and he told me a horrific story about one of his combat buddies. After one battle, he went back to find his buddy and found his friend in an indescribable position. This former soldier struggled to use words to describe what he saw." As he and Charles sat in the marble reflection of the Memorial, they both succumbed to tears and silence.[2]

Years ago I sat on a couch with a work colleague and friend as she waited for her husband to come home. He worked on the eighty-third floor of the second of the World Trade Center Twin Towers, and he never did come through the front door that day. My friend had candles lit on the door step and her whole church and community were praying, some even said her husband had been spotted in one of the hospitals in the confusion of the aftermath, but nothing ever came of it. At her husband's memorial, she wore a vibrant color, and the men wore Hawaiian shirts; she said that any retaliative killing would not be done in her name. We just listened to this very young widow. We couldn't fix this.

Recently, a friend of mine in Australia buried her newly married son. She had already buried her husband. Cancer has taken so much out of her family. There are no words for this kind of pain.

In Pakistan, the Philippines, China, and Louisiana, there are disasters that take the lives of loved ones. When I first started writing this chapter, there were thirty-nine miners trapped deep in a mine in Chile. The radio was full of rescue and recovery talk. "Does anyone recover from such an ordeal?" asked the commentator. Then Japan had an earthquake and the resulting tsunami wave was devastating.

At our church,[3] we welcomed the arrival of another Haitian family—a year after the hurricane, their home is nonexistent. Rescued indeed, but far from recovered. I could go around the world sounding like the evening news and only pause the remote to ask, "Why?"

THE "WHY?" QUESTION

When my son, Mark, was diagnosed with a malignant brain tumor, there was no way I wanted to ask God, "Why?" There was nothing God could say to me that would cause me to go "Oh, OK. In that case…". There would never be an answer good enough to satisfy my "why" question, so I didn't even want to ask.

I knew, however, that God was God. The night after Mark's surgery, I stood by his bed, and every half hour a nurse would come in and wake him to ask him questions, and then he would go back to sleep. At three A.M., just standing there silently praying, I felt the presence of the Holy Spirit. I felt a holy presence come down the hall and stand by the bed. I "knew in my knower" that *the Lord* had come to watch my son and to bring comfort to us all. It was only for a brief moment, but I will never forget that experience.

Many, many mothers who have watched their children throughout a night like this can tell of similar experiences. Our God never slumbers or sleeps. I did not hear any audible word from the Father. What was there to say? We just needed Him near, and He was.

If you think you have to come up with all the answers, and you need an explanation for every hurt in the world as part of your recovery, let me suggest that you consider for a moment that answers may or may not be part of your recovery. You can stomp your feet all you want— your loving, heavenly Father may even hold you while you do just that—but you may never reach an understanding of "why?"

Evil exists. We have an enemy who hates us. Why did God allow this? There is nothing you can say that would make me understand or accept the right of evil. We can have a theological discussion, and we can remember the story of an angel thrown from Heaven, but I am just a human, and I cannot get my finite mind around an infinite God.

Knowing "why?" doesn't change things; and yet if we are to have maturity, to be what we are meant to be as "overcomers," we still need to recover from whatever has damaged our spirit, soul, or body.

Psalm 22

At a recent Celebrate Recovery class in the United States, Pastor Charles Rowley read Psalm 22 aloud, in The Message[4] Version of the Bible. It starts out: My God, my God, why have You forsaken me?

"Sound familiar?" asked Charles.

The psalmist goes on to ask God, "Why are You so far from helping me?" There is a cry in the night as he calls desperately to the Lord. Here is what Charles read in entirety.

> God, God…my God! Why did You dump me miles from nowhere?
> Doubled up with pain, I call to God all the day long. No answer. Nothing.
> I keep at it all night, tossing and turning.
> And You! Are You indifferent, above it all,
> leaning back on the cushions of Israel's praise?
> We know You were there for our parents: they cried for Your help and You gave it; they trusted and lived a good life.
> And here I am, a nothing—an earthworm,
> something to step on, to squash.
> Everyone pokes fun at me;
> they make faces at me, they shake their heads:
> "Let's see how God handles this one;
> Since God likes him so much, let Him help him!"
> And to think You were midwife at my birth,
> Setting me at my mother's breasts!
> When I left the womb You cradled me;
> Since the moment of birth You've been my God.
> Then You moved far away and trouble moved in next door.
> I need a neighbor.
> Herds of bulls come at me, the raging bulls stampede,
> Horns lowered, nostrils flaring, like a herd of buffalo on the move.
> I'm a bucket kicked over and spilled, every joint in my body has been pulled apart.
> My heart is a blob of melted wax in my gut.
> I'm dry as a bone, my tongue black and swollen.

They have laid me out for burial in the dirt.

Now packs of wild dogs come at me; thugs gang up on me.

They pin me and down hand and foot, and lock me in a cage—a bag

Of bones in a cage, stared at by every passerby.

They take my wallet and the shirt off my back,

And throw dice for my clothes.

You, God—don't put off my rescue!

Hurry and help me!

Don't let them cut my throat; don't let those mongrels devour me.

If You don't show up soon,

I'm done for—gored by the bulls,

Meat for the lions.

Here's the story I'll tell my friends when they come to worship,

And punctuate it with hallelujahs:

Shout hallelujah, you God-worshipers;

Give glory you, sons of Jacob;

Adore Him, you daughters of Israel.

He has never let you down,

Never looked the other way

When you were being kicked around.

He has never wandered off to do His own thing;

He has been right there, listening.

Here in this great gathering for worship

I have discovered this praise-life.

And I'll do what I promised right here

In front of the God-worshipers.

Down and outers sit at God's table

And eat their fill.

Everyone on the hunt for God is here, praising Him.

"Live it up, from head to toe."

Don't ever quit!"

From the four corners of the earth people are coming to their senses,

Are running back to God.

Long-lost families are falling on their faces before Him.

God has taken charge;

From now on He has the last word.

All the power-mongers are before Him—worshiping!

All the poor and powerless, too—worshiping!

Along with those who never got it together—worshiping!

Our children and their children will get in on this

As the word is passed along from parent to child.

Babies not yet conceived will hear the good news—that God does what He says.

Charles pointed out that something changes three quarters of the way through the psalm. There is an attitude change, from outrage to praise. There must have been a miracle? Someone showed up and saved the day? No. Nothing happened, yet there is a marked change in verse twenty-two. One moment, the writer is calling out to God demanding to know where He is in all the mess and to save him from "the lion's mouth." In all desperation, he calls out to the Lord. Charles suggests that the very calling out is faith, and it is *in that faith* that something happens.

They shall praise the Lord who seek Him. In Hebrews 11:6 it says, "He rewards those who earnestly seek Him." In the midst of seeking and praising, something happens. There is a divine exchange, and it happens in our spirits. The exchange happens deep within, in your spirit.

Occasionally, holding on to the pain is all we have left of a loved one. I couldn't bear it when people said to me, "Oh, just give your son to the Lord." Are you kidding? You are talking to a *mom* here! Think tiger or angry momma bear who wants to stomp more than her feet to move Heaven and earth to sort out this cancer. You don't even think about calming down a momma bear in this state.

Then the Holy Spirit came down the hall with so much love in His eyes for my son that my loved paled by comparison. With tears softly flowing, knowing He held my heart so gently, I offered my prayer, "No competition, Lord...he's yours." In my spirit, I could lay my beloved son in His arms and look at the love between them.

He Becomes the Answer

When we try to work out for ourselves what is disturbed in our soul, our minds find it a challenge to gain answers that would satisfy. No human answer is good enough or sustainable. We can and must renew our minds, but there is nothing outside the work of the Holy Spirit that brings the healing of our minds, our wills, and our emotions.

We cannot undo or deny the reality of pain, though many have tried. My husband went to work that day our son was operated on for brain cancer. I do not blame him. What more could he do? Worry and pacing the halls wouldn't help; and besides, his wife was walking around the day room embarrassingly speaking in tongues. There is no right or wrong way to react to cancer. We all have to give each other some space for grace. The only thing that is not helpful to do, even though it is tempting, is to deny the reality.

Let me say that when you are a part-German family such as I am, you know there are those who would even deny the holocaust, just as some of us deny the violence of a childhood or find that accepting the death of a loved one is a long time coming.

For many Christians, facing the end of a marriage is more than we can bear. Divorce, even the breakdown of family communication or the loss of love, was never meant to happen to Christians. We weren't meant to have dead marriages. We were meant to have a strong family life that would establish strong communities. We were meant to have life to the full.

A Door Open

While I do not know what was open to the enemy to let in cancer, and I may not know this side of Heaven, the Lord did eventually bring me to an understanding of what brought my marriage into distress. This understanding hasn't brought me to pointing a finger as part of a blame game, but to an understanding of where I went wrong and how I can change what I do in the future.

In my case, I have to admit that the Holy Spirit tried to tell me not to marry my first husband. I didn't listen. While the Bible says that "what God has joined together, let man not separate," my husband and I put ourselves together. If we had had understanding at the time of our marriage falling apart, could we have gone before the Lord in repentance and asked Him to forgive us? I believe we could have done just that, but neither of us had teaching on "rescuing marriages that had begun in disobedience."

We were *meant* to have the teaching that would have bound up our broken family; instead we had a church who knew exactly how to fast and pray for cancer or other physical ailments, but no idea how to recover a marriage in distress. The shepherds themselves had not had the training. They were good people, but they did not know what to do.

A friend of mine recently endured an unwanted divorce; and bewildered from seeing so much divorce in her community, she asked, "Why is this happening, especially in Christian families? Is there some epidemic going on?"

Many families can and will be helped if they are blessed to be in churches where the shepherd is bold to obey the words of Ezekiel and seek the broken. To *prevent* the mounting evil dominating this world, we would ask that Adam had not sinned, nor Eve; but we give thanks that God was and is passionate about His people to send a Savior.

Jesus is that Savior; and as He forgives, restores, and heals, He enables us to share the deep well of living water. The door I had opened was disobedience to the Father's ways of living. I now needed to ask the Father's forgiveness for even thinking my way of living was better than His way, and shut that door.

The new door to be opened is to let grace in, the Lord's quite amazing, extravagant grace of forgiveness and the promise He will not tire of telling me about His Kingdom ways of living.

In the pre-dawn hours at Southampton General Neuroncology ward, my son awoke to the sound of a nurse asking questions such as, "Who is the Prime Minister of Britain?" and my son answering, "Who would you like it to be?" The nurse laughed, "He's getting better."

My son turned to me, "Mum! What are you doing here? Mum, I'm fine. Remember my verse? What is my verse, Mum?" He smiled kindly but he wasn't kidding. He wanted me to recite his verse out loud.

"To live is Christ, to die is gain."

"Right. Go get some coffee, Mum."

WOUNDED HEALERS

It has been awhile since I've been back to Pierrepont and Ellel Ministries Teaching hospital. I have so many fond memories of meeting Christians from around the world there. "Wounded healers," we often called those who reached that understanding that only the Father God Almighty heals, but that we must more than ever in these times be about our Father's business.

We need to share the good news. Ezekiel 34:17 reminds us that it isn't all down to the shepherds. We, the sheep of His pasture, must not keep this high healing pasture to ourselves. We are to be just as responsible as the shepherds to share the news that our God is the One who hears. The word "hear" in the Greek translation means "hear to respond."[5] Our God is not someone who just hears our cry and then remains unmoved. He has heard our cry and is adamant that those whom He sends in His name are to respond *along with* the moving and shaking He brings to the world.

Val is one of the graduates of NETS, and she now passes on what she has learned to others as she flies in on little planes to the Congo to bring the good news to hard-to-reach villages. Praise God for Mission Aviation Fellowship! What would we do without highly skilled men and women who maintain and fly airplanes to back country landing strips.

Judy, an Ellel prayer minister who, you may recall, taught me a thing or two on how to be a prayer warrior, uses her vacation time to visit and teach a people God has taught her to love, former members of the Sudanese Liberation army. She has a profound love for the Sudan and the people who struggle there to come into the freedom that Christ offers.

Others may lead a more pedestrian life, yet Christian life is never for the faint-hearted. If you want an adventure, you have never seen one until you receive one personally written for your life by the Father. There are stories from the Upper East Side of New York City to small towns in Mongolia. As we gain this key teaching that Father God is passionate about healing and restoring His people, we see He is working to teach us all to recover from the enemy's work in this world.

We need to see that it isn't just the formation of a subject called psychology that people have begun to gain understanding of healing broken individuals in a messed up world. We see from Genesis that the Father has been looking for man and woman since they left the Garden. We see from Ezekiel that He is passionate about searching out the lost and doing something about bringing them to His healing place, His high pasture for restoration. Read Ezekiel 34 once again, and you will see that the Father does not mince words.[6]

No matter what you are going through, what you have done in the past or had done to you, whatever the sin or wounding, the Father can recover the crushing in your spirit and the destruction to your mind, will, and emotions. Step by step, in the reality of dealing with anger, in the morning hours of seeking Him, and in allowing a divine exchange as we see in Psalm 22, you too can come to the high pasture.

Body, Soul, and Spirit Becomes Spirit, Soul, and Body

As we are going through difficult times, we often talk about or at least think about "our needs." One person in the Family Recovery course I taught in the United Kingdom said that all through the time of her family falling apart she was simply "hungry." She wanted comfort food!

Sometimes we have to laugh at our own foolishness in what we turn to in our hours of turmoil. My mother often said there wasn't much Dairy Queen (ice cream) couldn't solve. Got a problem? Having a bad day? Life has no joy? Hmmm, let's see. What am I hungry for?

With food addictions being one of the most socially acceptable addictions,[7] our family has often laughed over this "run to Krispy Kreme donuts" in stressful situations. When does a treat become not a treat? Oh, when it is a lifestyle.

The Bible is full of feasting,[8] but it was more as a celebratory event, or symbolic of deep communion. When food is taken as His body, broken for you and for me, then there is healing; but our own personal, earthly body was never meant to be in control or led to the food counter by our emotions. Paul cautions us to not let ourselves become slaves to our bodily needs.[9]

THE DIVINE EXCHANGE

When The Father calls us to a "Psalm 22 Moment," when we bring our broken world to His cross, there is a divine exchange.

> Our crushed spirit for His wholeness.
>
> Our damaged spirit for His healing.
>
> Our timid spirit for His boldness.
>
> Our starved spirit for His feeding.
>
> Our imprisoned spirit for His freedom.
>
> Our orphaned spirit for His parenting.
>
> Our defiled spirit for His washing and cleansing.
>
> Our broken spirit for His Spirit-to-spirit connecting.

THE MUSIC

Long before I had any idea as to the damaged condition of my spirit, I heard the audible voice of the gentle Holy Spirit say that He would use music to heal me. The Holy Spirit would lead me to the music that would enable me to step over the wall of hostility (see Chapter 6) and into the high pasture (Chapter 7). There by the still water He would restore my soul with resonating notes that would enable my mind, will, and emotions to be still and know that He is God.

The stirring in my spirit led me to know that He intended that I put a boundary around what I did on my Sabbath, and keep the Sabbath holy by attending a church that had what was for me, restoring music. (Even later, as my sabbatical came to a close, the Sabbath would remain a day of worship and recovery.) During the week, I would sing around the house and put on worship music to vacuum and clean. I can't pretend that dusting became a joy, but I enjoyed the music. I found Christian radio stations, and I downloaded CDs; but quite frankly, people just started giving me music.

As part of my healing journey in the high pasture, God gave me the opportunity to become a Christian radio announcer where I could play music throughout the show. In the New Wine breakfast show in Shepton Mallet, Somerset, United Kingdom, I would wake people up with music and the words, "It's a choice to rejoice!" One of the New Wine leaders joked that upon hearing me say this one rainy, tent-soaked morning, he was just about ready to take the radio and toss it! (People gaining the joy of the Lord aren't always a joy!)

Father God spoke to me once again about Saturday nights, where I would put a boundary around my time and we (God and I) would have a date night—soaking in the music just the two of us. There were times when a song would stop me in my tracks. I would stand there in the middle of my room, unable to do anything but weep as I heard the music. I made my bed to music, and I ate my dinner to music—and music began to calm me down (see Zeph. 3:17).

Music made it possible for me to be still and know even more He was God.

The music I listened to wasn't all worship music, but I knew it was music He wanted me to hear. Beethoven and Handel began to seep into play. I downloaded iTunes and walked with this music and slept with this music.

Even more healing came when the Lord gave me an opportunity, which by now I was ready to take, to apologize to my musician mother for my chaotic, rebellious years, for being so horrible about piano practice, in particular, and music in general. She forgave me for not receiving the only way she truly knew how to connect with me. We cried together, and it healed something, though I'm not sure what. Still, I felt a little stronger in the core of me for having asked and received forgiveness.

Then I attended chapel with my mother at her independent living "retirement home," where Mom played the piano every Thursday. I helped her find the pages in the Old Baptist Hymnal (as this was a Methodist Home we both ask your forgiveness). At eighty-nine years of age, Mom started finding it a challenge to play, but she determinedly persevered. In addition to chapel on Thursdays, a number of ladies and gentlemen at the Wesley Pines Retirement and Nursing Home had come to expect they could "have a little concert" on Mom's practice nights. They would sit down the hall in the lounge and with the chapel door open they would listen to her. On the day she said, "I can no longer play," I sat at the piano stool, with Mom in a chair beside me, and commenced struggling with "How Great Thou Art." I nearly wept as I was so dreadful, butchering this old faithful song, but Mom kept saying, "You're doing great."

When we walked out of the chapel that evening, her fan club was sitting there. "So good hearing you, Libby," they said and smiled at my mom. "It wasn't me tonight," she said, "It was my daughter."

"Like mother, like daughter," they said, and I gave thanks for ears that were deaf to my faults.

Our Course for Eternity

It is in the high pasture, at the foot of the cross, where the divine exchange takes place. This is healing for eternity, not a microwave moment to make us feel better this weekend but so that we can honestly say, "Thy Kingdom come, My will be done...on earth, as it is in Heaven." From this high pasture time we will one day gain the words that define our eternity, "Well done thy good and faithful servant," so that we can forever live in His Kingdom.

We will know that we have become an overcomer by the word of our mouths and "the blood of the Lamb" (Rev. 12:11). By the work and Word of the Lord, we are over the wall and in the high healing pasture, and the boundaries are set for living a life in His Kingdom. This was music to my ears.

But if I thought my high healing pasture was to be a cozy little nest complete with soundtrack, then I needed to think again.

The Father was about to flip me out of the nest to fly a little.

Chapter 10

THY KINGDOM COME

I suppose I should have realized that this recovery sabbatical couldn't go on forever. I was just about to ask God for an extension so I could learn more about what was meant by "kingdom living," when the news came.

My mother had ten days to live; and once again in our family, it was brain cancer. I was in Florida at the time, so I did what any Floridian would do, I headed down to the beach to have an argument with God.

I was angry to say the least. It had only been recently that my mother and I had any reconciliation. I was finally getting a mother, just when I was to lose her. I thought back to the Pierrepont anger class. I would kick sand.

I took one of those Styrofoam floating noodles and just beat the waves. I was beside myself with anger. I wanted time to figure this woman out, my mother; to have time with her, to hear she loved me. *Why, God, why take her now?*

And I didn't want an answer. I wanted to be angry. I wanted Father God to know just how angry I was. Couldn't she hang around long enough while I finished up my sabbatical year so I could come home all healed and restored to a Christian life that I could share with my family? I wanted my brother and sister to know all I had learned, so they too could find a high healing pasture for their lives. I didn't want go to my family with still so much to heal.

"Not yet, Lord, I have more to learn! You can't cut my sabbatical short!"

Oh, but He could.

And He did.

As much as I wanted to tell the Father about all the classes I wanted to attend when I got back to the United Kingdom and the Christian workshops that would be just what I needed to gain knowledge for growing in ministry, I sensed it would be a wasted conversation.

I packed my bags. I headed to North Carolina to be with my mother.

ON THE PORCH

My sister and I sat on the little porch at my mother's home in Wesley Pines Retirement Center in Lumberton, North Carolina. If ever there was a place far from the major churches with world-renowned speakers and colleges of theology, this would be it. I had been running in circles where bold Christians entered tribal warfare and brought peace. I had been inspired by being part of a church with a team that moved into the east end of London and lived among Muslims. I had been trained by Christians who stood on street corners and worked with prostitutes and faced up to drug addictions. Now I was back in a town with two Baptist churches, one White and one Black.[1]

Where I had lived in London and worked in New York City, I had major opportunities to learn that the crisis of divorce, my mess as I called it, could, through God's divine exchange, become a ministry. When my family fell apart, I had spent time at Pierrepont recovering, restoring my spirit, learning about healing and spiritual warfare, and I wanted a bold mission of my own—*but* suddenly God took me out of this arena. I felt as if I had been taken out of the classroom and sent home!

Now my sister and I sat with Mom, and the three of us looked at her doctor. It was a warm Carolina night, and Doctor B, as we lovingly call her, once again described the brain tumor that would soon take our mother's life. Doctor B finished explaining the biology and looked at my sister and at me.

"You girls are so privileged to have such a mother. She loves the Lord. She has taught you how to live," the doctor said.

And then she turned to my mother. "Libby…you are now, as their mother, going to teach these girls how to die."

Just like that. She said the words with such love and gentleness, but also with clarity, which made me suddenly realize that I was on sacred ground. I was humbled by this new classroom.

"Let's pray," said Dr. B. And so we sat on the porch, with a little breeze from the pine trees just outside, and we held hands and we prayed.

When we finished praying, Dr. B got up to head home. "So Kathy, what have you been doing in England?"

"Oh this and that…" I answered.

EXTRAVAGANT GRACE

Maybe God wanted to show me His high healing pasture was anywhere and everywhere. Maybe He wanted to also show me that He would spare no expense when it came to bringing a wealth of teaching if I would go where He would send me, even if that meant going to my mother's front porch.

As my sister, brother, and I cared for our mother, there wasn't much time for reading or attending lectures. I had no way, in the natural sense, to keep up with the latest teaching or even be aware if major Christian speakers would be coming to the nearest big town. I now rearranged my focus to be all the Lord wanted me to be for my mother, and to learn all He wanted me to learn at this time.

Funnily enough, He once again seemed to be showing me that when the focus was on Him, He could do anything. I had learned this while in the "teaching hospital," the loving nest where I had come to His high healing pasture, and now He seemed to want to teach me that His teaching would go on even if I was out of the nest. I am not saying I was soaring like the proverbial eagle that soars with knowing that God can do all things for my good, but I fluttered my wings a little with His next life lesson. By being literally right where I was at that very time, I had the opportunity to attend a seminar by one of my all-time favorite teachers, Dr. Myles Munroe. Oh, and Dr. Munroe flew in on a private jet to get to our neck of the woods.

I was helping my mother walk down the hall of the nursing section of Wesley Pines, when she needed to stop to catch her breath… just in front of the poster announcing that Dr. Myles Munroe was having a conference in an even more remote but nearby town, St. Paul, North Carolina. God also arranged it that my sister was available to look after Mom that night and that a good friend from our local Christian bookstore, Debbie Williams and her husband, could take me to the event.

Even Mom told me to go. She wasn't about to die in the ten days she had been told she had; she was planning a road trip to see her sister, and she had phone calls to make. So off I went for two nights of receiving the teaching I needed—Kingdom Living by Dr. Myles Munroe.

THE KINGDOM OF GOD

That night, somewhere on a back road of North Carolina (even Dr. Munroe admitted he didn't know exactly where he was and due to the bad weather he was just glad the plane had successfully landed), Dr. Munroe taught us that life is not in the pit, where we all sit and discuss life *out there*, as if it were some far-off dreamland where someone, somewhere, someday, is sipping milk and honey.

He reminded us that though we have not a passport, nor a visible sign of (not yet anyway) being subject to this Kingdom, Luke 12:22 tells us to not be afraid, "for your Father [the King!] has been pleased to give you the kingdom."[2] The King wants you in His Kingdom! There are no illegal aliens in the Kingdom of God. There is a gate at the border, but it is your heart and mind that will be screened, not your body.

Dr. Munroe, in his book, *Kingdom Principles*, tells us, "The moment we turn from our rebellion against God and place our trust in Christ to salvage us from the consequences of that rebellion, we become naturalized citizens of the Kingdom of heaven, with all the rights, benefits, and privileges that come with it."[3]

He went on to challenge us, "But if you are not *experiencing* the overcoming Kingdom life; there is, indeed, a problem to be solved."

It isn't that suddenly our marriage will be restored or our children returned to us, or reconciliation established in our family, we may rightly be in a Kingdom battle for all of this list, but he challenged us that we "should even now be living a life that inspires others." We have a right to be what Dr. Munroe describes as "operating on a level that blows other people's minds."[4]

And if that isn't happening?

"Most believers," says Dr. Munroe, "lack a proper Kingdom mindset. Life in the Kingdom is really about returning to the governing authority of God in the earth and learning how to live and function in that authority.[5]

AMBASSADORS FOR THE KINGDOM

And so it was with this teaching on Kingdom living, as much from the fact that I had a Father God who could and would arrange for me to have and know all I needed to live this life He died for me to have (including bringing into my awareness a teacher flying in on a jet on a dark and rainy night), as well as the content of the teaching, that I made a decision that night. I wanted to be an ambassador for God.

When I was back to night and early morning duty with Mom, I had time to wonder what kind of ambassador I could be. Dr. Munroe had inspired me to study even more this concept of Kingdom living; to know and love the land that would be mine for eternity. But what did it look like to be an ambassador?

Settling down for a few hours sleep, I recalled one ambassador who very much believed in the ordinary power of the Christian life. He had rolled up his shirt sleeves and had not stood on ceremony; he thought of unique ways to reach people, a people subject to a queen.

MR. AMBASSADOR TO THE COURT OF ST JAMES

For a while I was involved in the women's group at the American Church in London. Our leader, Susan (not her real name) was an inspiration, and from her we learned what it meant to come together to pray for our life as mothers and as wives, even if we had "titles to impress" at work. Susan was the one who taught me the importance of prayer partners and praying purposefully for my children.

She led by example. Susan's prayer partner, Linda Lader,[6] was quite an inspiration herself as she was the stepdaughter of Catherine Marshall (the author and wife of the former U.S. Senate Chaplain, Peter Marshall). Linda was also the wife of the United States Ambassador to the Court of Saint James; in other words, the American ambassador to England—and Susan invited her to speak to our group.

We all gathered at a member's home—a member who had the largest living room—and even then we sat on the floor and the arms of chairs to hear what the Ambassador's wife had to say to us. I arrived early that morning as I was on duty to help with setting out the food on the dining room table.

When I walked into the kitchen, I saw an unfamiliar American lady. I introduced myself and then plunged my hands deep into dish water. Quickly, this woman came with a tea towel and started drying cups and taking them to the table.

"How long have you been here?" I asked the question of any new arrival to London. I was used to being the Lehman Brothers Human Relations consultant for new families and even now thought I was a one woman welcome committee.

"A couple of months, but it has been chaos with unpacking and then my husband getting started in his new job...and I've hardly been anywhere that was really for 'me.' So I am looking forward to this morning."

"I am too," I said. "Has our speaker arrived?"

"Oh, I'm your speaker," the woman responded.

This was impressive and said much about her—meeting the ambassador's wife while washing dishes—but what she said in her talk will always stay with me. She spoke of how her husband was looking for ways to get to know the British people while living in "this fair land of Queen Elizabeth II." How would he get to know her subjects? Apparently he thought long and hard, and then came up with a plan.

He liked to hike. So he and a group of men hiked the length and breadth of the country, from Land's End up to John O'Groats. Linda Lader described in her talk just how he did it. Without a limo in sight, he and the men did the country in segments, every free weekend they had.

They wore jeans and lumberjack shirts and looked like ordinary guys out hiking the countryside. They stopped at pubs and spent quite some time getting to know the pub owners, the men with the "local knowledge" they would say. They enjoyed learning about the local food and drink and making new friends along the way. They did not let on to the pub owners, the landlords as many were called, that they were from the embassy, though it was obvious to all that some were Americans.

The publicans only found out later that they had made friends with the official United States ambassador when a very large, gilt-edged, engraved invitation arrived one day inviting them to be part of the British contingent at the ambassador's Fourth of July celebration in London. He had seen their land and how they lived. He'd made friends, loved their stories, and wanted to share a little of his own hospitality.[7]

It seemed to me that this ambassador fully believed in the power of the ordinary life. He was a Christian just doing his job, but what an impact it made on local people. As I thought again about the godly heritage of Linda, his wife, I began to wonder *how I could take inspiration* from all I had heard and seen, to be an ambassador for the Kingdom of God.

"But," I said to Father God as I prayed, "You would need to give me an assignment. Every ambassador has an assignment."

Chapter 11

FREQUENT FLYER

Be self-controlled and alert. Your enemy the devil prowls around like a warring lion looking for someone to devour. Resist him, standing firm in the faith because you know that your brothers throughout the world are undergoing the same kind of sufferings (1 Peter 5:8-9).

At the beginning of the film, *Love Actually*, Hugh Grant says that if we ever doubt there is any love left in the world we just need to go to the arrivals lounge at Heathrow airport. With scenes that depict parents reuniting with children, husbands and wives, we see young and old embrace as they reconnect. There is yet love in the world, if only as we fly in and as we fly out.

"Whenever I get gloomy with the state of the world," says Hugh, "I think about the arrivals gate at Heathrow airport. General opinion has started to make out that we live in a world of hatred and greed. I don't see that. Seems to me that love is everywhere. Often it's not particularly dignified or newsworthy but it's always there. Fathers and sons, mothers and daughters, husbands and wives, boyfriends, girlfriends, old friends. When the planes hit the Twin Towers, as far as I know, none of the phone calls from people on board were messages of hate or revenge, they were all messages of love. If you look for it, I've got a sneaky feeling you'll find that love actually is all around."[1]

FLYING IN

Carrie was flying into Tampa, Florida, to see me. If ever there was a "bolter" like me or like I used to be, it was Carrie. When life was painful, we both liked to leave the room, phone a friend, or even get on a plane. We could run away, any time, all the time. At the moment, Carrie was running away from the opinion of several friends and the leadership team at her church.

As I was the one who had led her to "accepting Jesus" (back in our divorce recovery class), she said; she needed to discuss her "new man, with someone who would be understanding."

"It is urgent," she said, as a way of explanation for spending a huge amount of money she did not have to fly from England to America. Maxing the credit card also reminded me of me; but I knew if she didn't bolt to see me in Florida, she would bolt somewhere else. I did want to meet with her.

I explained to Carrie that I was in Florida to look after my American mother whom my brother and sister had brought to be near me for care in, what even my mother was now admitting were her final days in a battle with cancer. If Carrie wanted to talk, she would need to come to me and sit quietly on the balcony of my mother's room at a place called Village on the Isle, about two hours south of Tampa. There would be plenty of time for us to talk, but it would need to be where I could keep at least one eye on my bedridden mother. Carrie agreed.

On a warm but balmy afternoon, Carrie arrived at the door of my mother's room. With joy we hugged; and with a finger to my lips suggesting quiet, we tiptoed past my mother and on to the balcony. Carrie smiled looking at the palm trees, but as I shut the balcony door, she offered sympathy for what I was going through in losing my mother.

"How are you doing?" she asked.

"The 'how' I am not sure about, but 'what' I am doing is creating what our Hospice[2] social worker calls a 'sacred space' for my mother. In the evenings we listen to the music she loves. I read to her during the day. Her favorite colors surround her. My sister, brother, and I speak as gently and quietly as we can, and the Hospice nurses are teaching us so much about the process of dying. We are learning how to say goodbye to her."

"Sounds like an amazing experience," Carrie said as she glanced through the window back into the room where my mother slept. She seemed to suddenly realize what she had walked into, a room with a dying person.

"Daily I check the nurses for wings," I said, motioning her to sit on a lounge chair. "They have been like comforting angels to Mom and to me." Maybe I needed to talk as much as she did. I felt full of "death stories," as people do when alongside someone going through this valley. I wanted to tell Carrie a story one of the nurses had told me, of how a tough New York cop was dying. He had said that the nurse's quest to see what faith he had about afterlife was "useless." He had "seen it all," he said, "more ugliness of this world, more terror, hurt and pain to believe there ever could be a God, much less a Heaven." Repeatedly he said, "I've seen too much to believe."

"And I," said the nurse, just as old and adamant as he was, "have seen too much to *not* believe."

"What d'ya mean?" asked the policeman, grappling with pain.

"I've worked with dying people for years and years," said the nurse. "I've seen the difference between those who believe in God and those who don't. They die differently."

I was full of these stories, and I wanted to share them with Carrie. The death experience of my mother was such a learning curve for me. The fact that my mom and I had had a reconciliation, forgiveness moments, and even words of love, was a testimony to what the Holy Spirit had done in my spirit. My mother had even blessed me with her hymn book, the one she used to play for chapel on Thursdays. So much God had done in my life to bring me to where I could care for my mother with compassion in her last days; and that compassion filled me to such a point that the nurses were surprised that she and I had ever had a rift in our relationship.

"Too many people die alone," the saints of Hospice and the nurses of The Village on the Isle Assisted Living[3] had said. They were amazed at the love I shared with my mom, and the love they saw in my sister and brother. They were even more amazed when I shared my rebellious teenage ways and how mom had never given up on me. When I had run away from home, she prayed for me. When I didn't want to bother with church, she prayed for me. When I divorced, she prayed for me. She wasn't perfect, but she prayed. God's Word and my mother's prayer of that Word in the lives of all her family had made a difference. It was the least I could do, to care for her in her last hours.

"Well, not everyone feels that way," the nurses had said.

But Carrie didn't want to hear any of this. "Someday," she said, she would "love to hear" my story. She was sitting on the balcony to tell me about her new man.

"But first," she said with a smile, "tell me how you met *your* new man!"

"I thought everyone at church knew that story. Carrie, you attended our wedding."

"Tell me again, please."

I sensed she wanted reassurance about being a Christian and getting married again. Can a Christian remarry? I left Carrie for a moment to check on my mother, but I also wanted to buy some thinking time. I prayed that the Father would enable me to tell Carrie about His second chance in my life. I walked around my mom's room and then back out on the balcony. I handed Carrie a cool drink and put my feet up on the stool. "You remember my accountability partner, Leslie?" I asked.[4]

"Yes, I remember, and I will have you know I am thinking about getting one of those prayer partners," said Carrie.

I laughed, but thought to myself that Carrie seemed to reflect so little foundational teaching in Christian living.

"Well, Leslie first introduced me to Ellel Ministries," I said to Carrie. "We were driving out to the retreat center when Leslie asked me about the ring I was wearing. 'It's my purity ring,' I told her. 'After my divorce, I wore that ring on my left hand as a reminder to me that I was *engaged* to be the Bride of Christ. I no longer lived as the pagans lived.[5]

I had made a decision to never, ever again compromise on the teachings of Jesus Christ for my life. I think I'm a nun,' I said to Leslie."

"'You are *so not* a nun!' Leslie had said, trying to drive and not be taken off track by my conversation."

I wasn't about to tell Carrie the whole long story, but what I did share was that I knew on that day God had a breakthrough for me.

"And what do you mean by 'breakthrough'?" Carrie asked as if hearing the concept for the first time.

"He finally gets through to me about something! I *finally* 'get understanding'⁶ on a matter. And on that day I realized that to be in His will, to live according to His Ways for my life, I would have to pass some tests. Each test would prove just how serious I was about living according to His Word, the Scriptures. These tests would be for my benefit; to show me my weakness for compromise. I would see where I was weak and needed strengthening, teaching, more of the Father's love. I was *determined* to not compromise on how I lived so that I could receive God's blessing on my life. I didn't want to block His blessing *of knowing His plan for my life.* Sometimes we can stop or block blessings the Father is longing to give us because we are not living in a manner He *can* bless."

Carrie nodded her head, but I'm not sure it was "OK, I hear you," or "OK, I understand what you are saying and agree."

"But you met your husband that day!" she said.

"Yes, I did. And I praise God that both of us were and are committed to a no compromise kind of life, where we seek understanding of how God wants us to live as husband and wife. I give thanks that we finally *got it* about what it means to be equally yoked⁷ and what it means to have a godly courtship, and to wait for your wedding night for sex. In our past, neither of us had understood just how serious the Father is about these things. They aren't optional extras to Christian living. Carrie, if you want God's blessings you have to do things His way. We had to make sure our marriage was His doing. When you marry without His approval, or even if you do have His approval but do not wait for His timing, or carry out the relationship in a way that honors Him, He doesn't have to show up when the tests of married life come."

I was stunned at the manner in which I spoke to Carrie. It was clear and concise, but why was there an underlying irritation? Who was I irritated with? Carrie? Myself? Maybe both of us; me, for taking so long to realize that God is not mocked in His teachings. We can't blame the 21st century and rationalize that God loves a good compromise. God's promise for marriage wasn't simply a discussion point where I could pick and choose which aspects of His plan for my life I would consider and accept. What was I thinking in my old life! How crazy could I have been?

And yet, that was exactly what I had done with my first marriage. I accepted the parts of God's ways for marriage that I liked, and ignored the parts I didn't like; rather like a bride-to-be selecting her flowers for her wedding. Star lilies, yes; carnations, no. Have a wedding, yes; wait to sleep together, no.

"So," Carrie said and then took a sip of her drink and looked straight at me. "You think it's OK to get married again?"

"I think it's OK to ask God *if you should* get married again and ask Him to give you a sign or a word so you have a clear answer," I said and looked right back at her. "It is *whatever God puts together* that no one should break apart. We often put ourselves together and then blame God when He doesn't show up and mend something He never made in the first place."

Carrie took a deep breath and then let it out. "I believe God has introduced me to the new man in my life. We plan to get married."

I didn't jump up and congratulate her. Something in her expression told me she was asking my opinion, wanting my approval. I had led her to accepting Jesus, and she seemed to think I must have an answer as whether or not to marry.

"Tell me about him," I said at last.

"He is a Christian before you hear anything else."

I knew in my spirit there was going to be a "but" somewhere. I was expecting, "He is a Christian, but he doesn't want to go to the same church" or "He is a Christian, but is recovering from an addiction"; but what she said next gave me such a sense of what can only be expressed as *dread*.

"His divorce hasn't come through yet."

I should not have been surprised, much less stunned. I should have just taken Carrie in my arms and like a big sister said, "Oh my sister, I am so sorry. Sorry because somewhere along the line I really messed up by not sharing the teaching that God is serious about marriage. I really messed up by not telling you the truth in love that the legal document of marriage is to be upheld and respected.[8] You could pray for his wife and pray for a restored family, but he is not free to date."

Why had I not told her? With the world in all its crazy ways of blending, defining, and cohabiting as family, how was she to know the justification of someone "applying for divorce" is not divorce? That satan is a legalist and there is no way he would miss a chance to use whatever we give him as a landing pad for damage to hearts and minds? She had opened a door that needed to be shut.[9]

One of the oldest tricks in the enemy's book is to use distraction, or the allure and enticement of someone, to take you away from Kingdom living—then when someone tries to tell you the Father's keys to godly living, the enemy whispers in your ear, "Did He really say that?"

I had been Carrie's "fat sheep,"[10] someone who knew the Shepherd and how to get to His high pasture; but instead of leading her to the truth of how we are to live when we turn to Jesus, I had left her as a new Christian to fend for herself. I didn't ensure that she would receive the discipling she would need. I hadn't kept the conversation going concerning what God had started in her life. Due to my own concerns, I hadn't taken the responsibility to see that she had made it into a flock, a faith family. I hadn't so much as looked back to see that she had made it to a high pasture for healing. It was indeed her responsibility to find or join a church that taught God's Word, but I hadn't even assisted her in seeking a church that provided an emotionally safe place for healing. With her upbringing, how was she to know what a safe place looked like?

And there was more.

What was worse, in a heartbeat I knew I had sold Carrie a bill of goods. That evening, an evening at a Divorce Recovery meeting that seemed long ago, I had heard her pain. Carrie had longed to see the healing we had in our lives happen in her life. When I knew she truly wanted an answer to the hope that was in me, I had told her only half the answer, sharing only the first part of the answer. The answer was, is, and always will be the *the* Shepherd, Jesus Christ; but I had used His name as a Buddhist would use a mantra or a New Age humanist focused thinking on the positive. Carrie had been desperate to get rid of the pain; and in my misled compassion, I had only told her the easy bit. I had given her the name of Jesus as if it were a band-aid.

It was as if I had said, "Here. Here is a Person who will make it better," and I never told her the whole truth. In essence, I had lied to Carrie. I might as well have said, "Here. Become a Christian and it will all be better. You'll feel better." I was like an irresponsible doctor who did not check the vital life signs, but instead said, "Here. Take two aspirin and you'll be fine in the morning." She wasn't fine in the morning!

Now I needed to say that there was a key to the presence of the Holy One. We needed a key to *dwell* there—not run away any more. If there was one place in the whole world we needed to stay it is in the shelter of the Father.[11] And the only way to stay in that place was through the key of brokenness—through repentance for the way we have lived. We needed to tell the Father that we are turning from (what we need to be acknowledging as) our wicked ways and *promise* there will be no turning back. We have to turn from the futility of how we have lived and determine to have deep remorse for how we have lived—not justification or excuses. We need *to call how we have lived,* "bold-faced sin."

In my shame, I asked God to forgive me for only telling Carrie about His Son and only telling her that she needed to accept Him, without explaining that she needed to know remorse for how she had lived without Him. Jesus wasn't just a quick fix for the pain we wanted to avoid. She needed to meet with Jesus, not just know He existed.

She needed to be sorry.

She needed to know that she was a sinner.

And I needed to be very sorry that I had been complicit in letting her think that she was a good person whose only need was to simply tack Jesus onto her life, and all would be well. She had just about zero foundation for a new life in Christ; and it was no wonder that, in confusion, she fled the moment she sensed disapproval from any corner.

Carrie had only, merely, been sad that she had had to live with pain, not remorse for her life of sin. Carrie had only wanted out of her pain pit, and I had not told her that the price of true freedom was accepting the fact that the sin she had committed, as well as the wounding from others, had put her in the pit in the first place. New life wasn't just accepting that Jesus had some good principles to live by, and try as you might to do your best to live by them you might/probably will fail; but hey, when you failed, didn't everyone come up short?

As we sat on the balcony, I didn't know what to do or to say to Carrie. I realized that because of me, she had a cheap conversion. She had not died to her old ways. I had been in the high pasture, a sheep of His flock, and I had trampled on the bits about repentance. Ezekiel 34:17 flashed across my mind. I hadn't told her that you have to be so sick of your old life and ways that you just want to die. You make a decision to let the old self go, and desire a new life, born again but this time birthed by the Holy Spirit.

I sat and looked at Carrie. There was nothing in her spirit that convicted her of dating a married man. She seemed to think that if she could get enough Christians to agree with her, whatever she did would be OK. Rather like checking with club rules to see if she could do something slightly unusual but not be kicked out of the club.

Out of the corner of my eye, I saw my mom stir. "Back in a minute, Carrie."

I went to my mother's bed, and pulled the cord for the nurse to come. I adjusted my mother's blanket, and held her thin hand. Looking at her perfectly formed, piano playing fingers, I wanted to ask her, "What do I say to Carrie, Mom? You would be good at this, listening and advising." The pain of losing a mother I had only recently regained gave me sorrow for the time wasted. My time wasted. She never thought her time of prayer and sticking with a child, no matter how stubborn, was wasted.

"Well, God," I said silently, "if I can't ask her, I am asking You. What on earth can I say to Carrie?"

A knock came at the door, one of those polite knocks from a person who knows he is most welcome and comes right on in. Lee (all of mom's nurses were her favorites so it was no point in saying this was the kind man that Mom just adored) checked her chart and then her pulse. He lifted the blanket gently to check her feet, and then tucked her in with a soft touch. Lee had explained to me that Hospice now had "these terrific mattresses" (he pointed to where Mom slept) where the patient doesn't need to be turned to avoid bed sores. Other things I had also learned, such as the blessing of anti-anxiety medicine that you rub on the wrists. Lee knew Mom wasn't a fan of injections. Hospice had a "no pain policy," when it came to dying. As one of the night nurses had taught me, "Pain, we can take care of; but suffering is optional—it's between you and the Lord." I am in awe of those Bible-belted nurses who don't mince words.

"Let's move your mom's bed a little," said Lee. "She loves the sunset, and with a little more over to the right we can position it for when she wakes up."

As I helped roll the bed, the voice I know and love as my Shepherd spoke to me. "Out of your brokenness," He said.

I almost let some tears come with gratitude to hear Him, but instead thanked Lee.

"I'll check on you later," he said, making a note on another chart. "You OK?"

"I'm hanging in," I said, smiling at my own recollection of American expressions and walked back out to the balcony.

Carrie had been on the phone and looking out at the palm trees.

Regretting my earlier tone, I said as gently as I could, "Carrie…I have a friend who had a dream, and she knew in her spirit this dream was from the Lord. In this dream she was told to stay faithful to her husband no matter what. In this dream, her husband was unfaithful to her but he would come back to her. In real life, not solely in a dream, he has not only had an affair with another woman, but has married someone else, divorced, and then went on to another affair. Through it all she has prayed and fasted and checked that what she heard and saw in that dream was from God, *truly* from Him."

"She's an idiot," said Carrie slightly laughing.

"Many of her friends who love her and see her broken heart would agree," I said and looked away beyond the palm trees to where I pictured whole families gathering to see a Gulf of Mexico sunset. I felt like having a good long run up and down the beach.

"But not you?" asked Carrie.

"Well, I have wondered. I have listened to what she has said and looked her straight in the eye and asked 'are you sure?' And I have come to the conclusion that on most days she is very sure and on some days she goes back to God and checks her own hearing. But *she knows,* in that place where you just know you have heard from God. And at the end of the day, she has—like everyone else—an appointment with the King. She will be the one standing before Him to answer to Him alone. No one else. Not me or anyone, just Him. She has to be faithful to what she hears from Him."

Carrie put down her glass, "I couldn't do that," she said.

"Well, I asked the Father if that was what He wanted *me* to do. You know, stay with my first husband. The answer was clearly 'no.' We all have to ask the Father, and then no matter what anyone else tries to tell us, we have to be faithful to what we hear. We will have to give account one day. We know we need to search the Scriptures as the Holy Spirit would never tell us to do anything that did not line up with the Word of God."

Just then my brother came into the room. He could see I was on the balcony with someone he didn't know so he waved and then went straight to Mom. He kissed her and sat on the edge of her bed, holding her hand. He too had taken the time to reconcile any past issues or differences with Mom. He was a support to his sisters, carrying a heavy load of suitcases to and from airports for visitors, shopping for all Mom needed, and then sending my sister and I off to get a facial or massage when he could see we were under stress. "How do you get a brother like that?" someone from our Florida church had asked.

"Look Carrie," again speaking gently, but this time I reached for her hand and not put off by her looking away from me, I said, "have you ever heard of Joyce Meyer[12] on TV?"

Carrie nodded, "I was thinking of downloading her podcast talks."

"Well, she tells this story of 'going around the mountain.' Each time God has a test for you, and you fail the test, you go around the mountain again until you get it right. If we are sorry we fail one of His tests and we confess, He forgives us…but we seem to face the test again."

Carrie wasn't impressed, and I was worried I was putting her off one of the best Bible teachers I have ever heard. When I was unable to attend teaching conferences or receive the help I needed from my local minister or connect with my own mother, Joyce had come into my home and made plain the path to freedom in the love of Christ. Her teachings had helped me understand. Her humility had taught me humility, and the laughter she brought had been good medicine.

"Brokenness," I heard the Holy Spirit say again.

"Oh yeah," I said aloud, "out of my brokenness."

"Pardon?" Carrie was looking at her watch. My sister had also come into Mom's room and joined my brother sitting with Mom. It looked as if Carrie was preparing to leave.

"Carrie, I promised God that I would not serve two masters when I gave my life to Him. When I married the first time, I totally failed. I was always struggling to serve two masters, one foot in the world and one foot trying to keep up with what I thought was my faith. I just broke. As I failed in my marriage and in all my dreams for my family, it broke me. Crushed, I cried for days over divorce papers. I cried when I understood God didn't want me to hold on as my friend had been told to hold on. I finally said, 'Father make me stronger or take me out.' In ways that were very clear to me, He took me out of the marriage, and I just fell apart. How could I be a Christian and divorce? I wanted to be a Christian hero who stood for her marriage against all odds, just like my friend. How could I face my children and call myself a Christian mother? Out of shame and complete brokenness—no pride but a faith that God was God—I made a quality decision that I would be obedient to what He said for my life. One moment, then one hour, then one day at a time.

"I knew He hated divorce; and He hated the disobedience that had brought me to that place of divorce, but I also knew He did not hate me. He loved me even if I couldn't at the time feel that love. With total disregard to my personal feelings of despair, or perhaps numb from feeling, I decided to take Him at His Word. I told Him if He didn't heal my pain or lift me out of the pit of despair, I would just remain in that pit. *Nothing and no person* would be allowed to take me out of that pain pit. Only Him.

"It was out of that *brokenness* that the Shepherd came to me and gently lifted me, one quiet moment at a time. I would have dreams, not dreams for strength to carry on, but dreams of Him washing me. He held me in a pool and with an alabaster jar He poured water over me. Carrie, with such love, I vowed to never again be in any relationship that He didn't design."

"And?" said Carrie, now looking straight at me.

"And from that time, He has led me out of brokenness into healing, step by step. I've searched the Scriptures...posted them all over my house so His Word was never out of my sight. There is so much love in His Word. But this can't be a story about what I did to get better, or what I did to meet someone new, or what I did to share a grain of healing with my family...the whole story is about Him loving me, not how I served Him. He loved me enough to tell me the truth. He loved me enough to put a boundary around how I live. He loved me enough to show me His nail-scarred hands and ask me if I was serious about intimacy with Him."

Carrie and I sat quietly for a moment. The Florida sky was developing another colorful sunset. It was a degree or two cooler now. Inside the room, I could see my sister turning on the little lamps that were next to my mother's bed. My brother got up to help a woman who was carrying a large instrument in the door.

"We are having a harp player this evening. It is quite a surprise. The Hospice office called this morning and arranged it. Can you believe that is someone's volunteer job?" I asked Carrie. "This is what she does…plays her beautiful instrument for those who are dying."

"If all these people are here right now," said Carrie, "won't you come with me for a short walk on the beach before I head back to the airport? It would do you good to get out for a while. I've got to meet Bill's plane…that's his name, Bill. I had hoped to introduce him to you but I think we will just stay in Tampa tonight. I've got a little time before I need to drive back."

I shook my head, "No, my friend. Carrie, do you know how hard it is for me to 'stay in the moment' as they say? I would love a walk on the beach, but I know beyond doubt I need to stay right here, with my mother and my family."

FLYING OUT

Carrie bid her farewells, giving me a hug and allowing me to introduce her to my sister and brother. "I am so sorry to intrude," she said and only allowed me to walk her as far as the elevator. I had no idea if I would see her again. I hadn't passed *her* test for being a good friend. As the elevator doors closed I mumbled something about praying for her, and then sadly and slowly walked back to my mother's room.

There in the low lamp light, and the pinks of the sky outside, the music began. The notes of "Be Still My Soul" played to the tune of Finlandia and we looked over the shoulder of the musician to read the words on her kindle. In a moment or two, my husband walked in with the dinner he had brought for all of us; and not far behind, was our Florida pastors Jim and Joy McInnes. How had our pastors known to come on such a night? Had my husband phoned them? "No," he said, "a little Divine appointment."

And so around the bed, my brother, sister, me, my husband, Jim, Joy, and the musician we had never met but felt we had always known, stretched out hands as Jim began to pray, "Father, we love this dear lady as she prepares to be with You. We thank You that any death of one of Your saints is precious to you;[13] and you have prepared a place[14] for her from the beginning of time."

As we sang my mother's favorite hymns, it wasn't just the Florida weather that made me take off my shoes. I was standing on sacred ground on an evening I could never have orchestrated, and knew I would remember this moment forever.

In the days ahead, Mom would tease about "her favorite nurse" bringing her black cherry ice cream. As she had glimpses of Heaven, she would say things like, "More than imagined!"

I would jump to her side, "What, Mom? What are you seeing?" Instantly I would suppose I understood what was happening to her and say things like, "Is it chocolate, Mom? Can you have all the chocolate you want now?"

And she would wave her hand as if to say, "Silly child"—but her words were, "New recipes. Things you can't imagine," and then she would smile.

"I love you," she said at last.

That's how she died, or "graduated," as members of her Bible class would say. She had this peace that was beyond *my* understanding. Jesus came quietly, early one morning; and by His love took her home. Her earthly assignment was complete.

> *I will give them an undivided heart and put a new spirit in them...and give them a heart of flesh.* **Then** *they will follow My decrees and be careful to keep My laws. They will be My people and I will be their God* (Ezekiel 11:19-20).

> *...They have eyes to see but do not see and they have ears to hear but do not hear, for they are a rebellious people* (Ezekiel 12:2).

Can't you be satisfied to drink from the clear stream without muddying the water with your feet? ...Because you forced your way with shoulder and rump and butted at all the weaker animals with your horns till you scattered them all over the hills. ...I'll put My Spirit in you and make it possible for you to do what I tell you and live by my commands. You'll once again live in the land I gave your ancestors. You'll be My people! I'll be your God! (Ezekiel 34:18,21; 36:24-28 TM)

Almighty God, unto whom all hearts be open, all desires known, and from whom no secrets are hid, cleanse the thoughts of our hearts by the inspirations of Thy Holy Spirit, that we may perfectly love Thee, and worthily magnify Thy Holy Name, through Christ our Lord. Amen.[15]

Chapter 12

THE BONE PICKER

He asked me, "Son of man, can these bones live?" (Ezekiel 37:3).

My cousin Danny was standing tall and quiet next to the grave site. Even without his uniform, this off-duty Marine looked like a Marine. Our family started to arrive to take their places at my mother's burial in the old, Charlotte cemetery; each one took a moment to hug Danny and say, "Welcome home, Soldier."

"Where was it this time?" some managed to say, "Afghanistan? Iraq?"

"Afghanistan, always Afghanistan. Not been to Iraq," he would say patiently.

My sister, brother, and I took our places as the violinist began to play Sebelius. We smiled at the accompanying noise of a train passing the graveyard. Our childhood vacations had been wrapped up in train journeys across the country, so it seemed fitting to have a reminder of Mom and Dad calling out to us, "All aboard!" at the start of each adventure. In every step of the way in this particular and personal journey of saying goodbye to Mom, God remained poignantly in the details.

Never for a moment did He leave us, constant were the reminders of how He loved to give visual cues and clues to what it meant to belong to Him. What we didn't know at the time but now have come to expect was that God would continue to send those postcards of care all our days. The service we were attending that morning was just a start to opening our eyes to a new stage of this life journey.

After the service, the family went for a meal in one of those Italian restaurants where the owners seem to have a life mission of getting families to eat together. They understood we had "just buried" our mother, and gave us a quiet back room. The waitresses came with care, soulful looks, and plenty of food. No one tried to make jokes or get us to laugh. Still, we did laugh and speak about childhood memories, and I took a moment to see if I could catch up with Danny.

"How's Sarah?" (not her real name) I asked about his wife who had not flown in from Texas to be with us at this time.

"She's OK," he said, but I thought he was looking a little too brave.

I looked right at him. "What does that mean?"

"Well, she couldn't come because of the kids."

"How are they?"

"Fine."

My husband sat down beside me at the table, and as we passed the bread and carafe of water around, I introduced him to Danny.

"You two have never met," I said, stating what they both knew.

It was just so good to be with family, around the table, talking about our lives that we never really get to share as we live in different states and different countries. My aunt and uncle presided over the table as the new elders, and we exchanged email addresses and phone numbers. There was a heartfelt desire to share more, but an almost defeatist understanding that, due to distance, we hardly knew where to begin.

As we were leaving, Danny had a quiet word with me. "Sarah and I may be separating," he said. I touched his arm and gave him a hug. I started to say, "I am so sorry," but he stopped me.

"We *may be* separating. I'm not sure. I hope not. Family means a lot to me...and...I told her about Kim" (not her real name). He shook his head, thinking about the little girl, his daughter he had in a relationship before he met and married Sarah.

"And she didn't know about Kim?" though I knew the answer to that one just looking at him.

"Sarah has gone to her mother's for a few days to think. This has all just blown up. Apparently, Aunt Libby wrote Kim a letter."

"That would be Mom!" I had to smile. "Having an impact on the family even after we've buried her. That's my mom, your aunt, all right. No secrets. Nothing hidden."

Danny moved to help the older relatives with their coats and walked his mother out to her car. He waved from a distance as my husband and I got ready to leave the restaurant. "I'll call you!"

And I called back, "And if you don't, I'll call YOU!"

But Marines always keep their word.

Family Reunions

For a long time I have believed most people leave family reunions with good intentions of staying connected. There may be a relative or two you would rather not see again, but most of us have a special place in our hearts for what we call family. Our family had become so disconnected that the tradition (for those families who did not "do life together") of family reunions, was a thing of the past. In a nuclear family sort of way, we had gathered for mom's 89th birthday; but mostly, we were down to being a "weddings and funerals" sort of family.

As my husband and I drove away from the Italian restaurant with its purpose-built family room, I remembered what the restaurant owner had said. "No Italian family would fit in this room! We need the whole restaurant!"

I pictured the hugs and the goodbyes of all of us in the foyer of our family gathering at lunch and another thought came to mind. It was a teaching from Ellel Ministry's Luke Nine Eleven Training School.[1] It had been one of the first lessons I learned in what I still refer to as "my year of recovery sabbatical." I recalled the words on one of the handouts, "We act on our beliefs."

"Which belief?" I asked in my spirit *for I just knew God was starting a conversation with me.*

"The one you just thought," were the words that came flooding from deep in my spirit into my mind. I knew this was the Voice of my Shepherd.

"The one about family reunions?" I always seem to have to ask for clarity even if my heart knows the answer.

"That would be the one...what do you believe *most people* think about family reunions?" He asked.

"Oh dear...I seem to at least be saying I believe that most people would like to attend family reunions and keep connected to the wider family."

"So who was missing from your family meal today? Who was not at the table?" The Holy Spirit spoke not with condemnation but with a pain He was hoping I would at least acknowledge. My husband, though now negotiating the urban streets of Charlotte, North Carolina, saw my tears and without a word reached over to hold my hand.

And then faces came to me. There was Cousin John (not his real name), in prison for drug dealing. At lunch we hadn't even acknowledged his existence. No one said, "Well, last week when I went to visit John, he said to send his love and he wished he could be with us. He remembers how much he loved his time with Mom on family vacations."

And then there was Cousin Julie (not her real name), a huge success at a Colorado university. She had found that being adopted into the family at birth just *didn't* enable her to overcome the craziness of living with what she labeled a "super religious family." She had stood through the terror of the night of an earthquake as a five-year-old child of missionaries (my aunt and uncle), and no one took care of her little traumatised heart. Every adult she knew toiled for hours to rescue their town in Chile, but missionary kids at that time were like cobbler's children.[2] Now she was too old to admit such things, and she covered the impact of being a missionary kid under a theological fight with her father. Having her at the table could have meant a war of words.

As name upon name came into my mind and I could see the faces of all who were missing, I am ashamed to say I felt *relief* at some of them not being there. I had enough emotion to deal with in transferring Mom's body from Florida back to where we traditionally buried members of our family in Charlotte.

My mother now joined five past generations of the family line in a historic Southern cemetery. It brought a sense of continuity and peace to see grave marker after grave marker of my forefathers; and I noted the civil war veteran, the grandfather who had established seven churches in Charlotte, the baby who died just days old a generation ago, but there were only so many members of the *present* generation I was prepared to tolerate even at a funeral.

I realized that I had to admit to the Father that it was *convenient* for me to believe a lie of how we "all loved to gather at this time." I seemed to believe somewhere in my mind that family reunions were a joy to all, and at the same time forget those who didn't have the courage for family communication. I believed a lie so that I didn't have to have the shame and pain and effort of loving all the people who were missing around the table, as well as the graveside. If I was honest, *I was glad* they weren't there! Maybe when they could be nice again, or come with a prison pardon, I could muster up a genuine welcome.

Yet I knew in *that place of my spirit and soul,* I was being handed something. I was gently being handed a powerful teaching from the Father. I also knew this teaching would be the very match for the life-changing words of Ezekiel 34, though at that moment I couldn't see the connection.

When Jill Southern Jones had read the chapter from Ezekiel to me, to the class, a passion had been ignited in my spirit for recovery ministry. Tears had streamed down my face and try as I might to choke back the emotion, the words of Ezekiel got through to me. These words were announcing, in a manner I had never seen or heard, that even if the earthly shepherds had not bothered to rescue *me* on my dark and cloudy day when my own family fell apart in the brokenness of divorce and under the battle of cancer, there was the Almighty God Himself who would head up the rescue team. I just needed to ask Him! He had a determination and a plan to rescue me! On that day in class, I finally got it that *no one* is to mess with a child of the living Lord! I was His child! His! Over a year earlier I had stood at my friend's window and saw a ball of wool somehow drifting across the sky and took that crazy artwork to be a sign from God. I had looked at that floating skywriting and just knew that the Father was telling me He would "do a new thing." I had to cast my care on Him as a child casts a messed up piece of knitting; at Ellel, I began to learn *His care* wasn't just my wishful thinking.

On the day I heard Jill read that Ezekiel chapter, I knew in a way I had never known that the living Lord was all about recovering the lost lives of His people. And it was personal! We are precious to Him. *He is* the rescue plan.

My mother hadn't even been buried twenty-four hours and through the cloud of grieving this loss, I knew that the audible voice of the living Lord was giving me what I thought of as an "impossible assignment" of telling people this very good news. He was telling me I *could have* a ministry of reconciliation, of at least in some small part addressing the mess that resulted from the attack of satan on godly family life in this world. It would need to start with my own family, but even if I didn't accept this larger "mission impossible" of sharing this life-giving news of hope, just knowing this plan of God the Father existed would challenge me for the rest of my earthly life. It was the *challenge* set out in Ezekiel, but it was the *ministry of the Messiah Jesus*. Jesus would take us beyond the brokenness to new life.

Scared, excited, grieving, I said "yes." Though I had no idea what the assignment truly entailed. I just knew He would teach me every step of the way. It was an assignment that would blow my mind; but before I did anything, I needed to know what on earth God was talking about.

Texas Grandmothers

As a result of Danny's call, I arrived the next week at his mother-in-law's house out in the back woods of Dallas. It was hard to get out as far as the back woods—more like the back desert—of this sprawling city, but with the help of the GPS on the rental car, I made it. Anna (not her real name) was sitting on the back porch, waiting for me.

Anna was Sarah's elderly mother. She was frail and feisty, and had that weathered-brown skin of a farmer's wife though her husband had died long ago and they had only an acre or two left of what used to be the farm. Her house wasn't too far from my own forefathers who had helped settled a little town south of Dallas called Cleburn. Anna hadn't been to Dallas itself, the proper city of Dallas, more than once or twice in her life. As I got to know her, I would learn that she didn't much care for city folk.

But now, I parked my car around the back of her house and as I got out from the long drive from the airport, I called out, "Hey, Anna!"

"Hey yourself, young lady," she said with that deep drawl of country.

Anna didn't stand up, and I seriously wondered if she was fit enough to stand or walk, but she said, "You want some pie? I made it fresh this morning."

I climbed the few steps, "Would you like me to get it?"

"No," she said. "You sit and rest yourself after all your travels. Did you come from England today?" I could see her smile. She seemed to know that for a good part of the year I live in the United Kingdom. How could she know so much about me, and I know nothing about this extended family member I was meeting for the first time?

As she quickly went in the house and let the screen door slam behind her, I saw the letter. It had my mother's last-stage-of-life handwriting, and I saw it said, "Dear Sarah."

"Did you see Sarah's letter?" asked Anna as her shaky little hand handed me a slice of peach pie with a scoop of ice cream.

The accompanying fork was looking a little precariously placed, so I grabbed it quickly. "That letter?" I said, pointing to the letter with the fork.

"Did you know your mother wrote it?"

"No," and I was thinking I didn't even know Mom knew Anna. Mom seemed to know quite a few people I had never heard of, and she kept in touch with them. Since her death, my sister, brother, and I had heard of Mom's weekly phone calls, cards, letters, and frequent visits from people around the globe who loved her. They all spoke of how Mom loved them.

Anna sat bolt upright. "Well, I'm going to tell you what it said. You can read it for yourself later. It says 'Dear Sarah, I have longed to talk to you and to see you once again. You are on my heart, and I can't get you out of my mind, not that I would want to. I miss you. You are important to me. You will have heard by now, that I have a brain tumor and do not have long to live. This news has been quite a shock to me, but I know where I am going. I am more concerned for you, that when it comes to the end of your life you might not know where one of the members—one of the precious people God has given us—of our own family is going. It is my dying wish that you would be strong enough to reach out to this person. Her name is Kim, and she is the child of your husband, my beloved nephew Danny. Secrets never helped anyone, and I hope we can talk before I die. I am trusting God that you will overlook sins of the past and reach out to this innocent child. She lives nearby. Your mom will give you her address. Remember, I love you and Danny. Love, Aunt Libby."

"Well that was to the point," I said to Anna.

"Texas women and dying men don't mess around, and they don't waste words," said Anna.

The chair I was sitting in rocked a little. I started rocking it more, saying nothing and just eating fresh, homemade peach pie. Had years of settled-down life meant I had lost a pioneering gumption? I had come to Texas with some noble aspiration to see if I could help Danny in his time of need, but it seemed my mother had made it clear I was out of my depth.

"Sorry about your mother," said Anna after a while. "She was a good woman."

When I put the plate down, Anna came over and put her arm around me.

SUNDAY MORNING

Danny's car suddenly appeared at the back of Anna's house. Leaving the car door wide open, he walked straight into the house, down the hall, and knocked on Anna's bedroom door. "Five minutes, ma'am! Get your war paint on and let's rock and roll."

I came out to the kitchen, all dressed for church. "I'm ready."

Danny gave me a hug. "And we meet again!"

I went out to his car, waiting for him to do what I had seen my uncles do in a past generation, taking the arm of an elderly lady relative and teasing her about being the most beautiful woman in Texas. Only recently my brother had taken the arm of my own mother and gently helped her into what I call "a Sunday morning car." (Sunday morning cars have had a Saturday morning clean!) My sister had done the same for Mom, Sunday after Sunday. Holding her handbag, her Bible (which Mom insisted on taking even after her eyesight had failed); her bits and pieces held at the side, one arm around Mom so that she wouldn't fall. I pictured elderly men and women all over the world being helped out of their rooms, their apartments, their homes and into a car or onto a bus and heading for church on the Sabbath. Maybe I would be hobbling down a step or two to someone's car in the years ahead.

"Where are Sarah and the kids?" I asked after we were down the drive and on the road.

"We'll meet them there," said Danny, but I knew something was up. I saw that somewhat cantankerous mother-in-law of his smiling.

CALL TO WORSHIP

Anna liked to sit in the same place every Sunday. "That way people know where to find me," she let me know. We got her to her place and sat down for a quiet moment before the start of the service. And that's when it happened. On an ordinary Sunday morning at an ordinary church service, an ordinary family gathered. I know I was still grieving my mother, but this profound sense of loss was overcome by a profound sense of gain as first I saw Sarah come and sit next to Danny and hold his hand. They kissed in a church-like way, but it was a kiss that bore no hint of imminent separation. Their kids—teenagers—had quickly come by to say "Hi!" to me and then ran to the back of the church to be with their friends. If I was blessed to see this family together, I hadn't begun to expect or understand what happened next.

Kim came and sat next to Sarah. This was Kim, the child born of another relationship sitting next to the wife of her father. And that wife was reaching over to this child of her husband's and giving her a hug. I shook my head in disbelief; did I hear Sarah actually say, "I love you, Kim"?

Then Kim's mother came and sat next to Kim. Being a "bolter from way back," I started looking around the sanctuary for an escape route in case there was a Texas brawl! Texas women don't take kindly to someone messing with their man, but here was Sarah handing Kim's mother a church bulletin and saying "Welcome!"

Then just when I thought I had seen about everything, Kim's stepfather came and sat next to Kim's mother, and I was not taking the Lord's name in vain when I whispered under my breath, "Oh Lord, have mercy!"

Then Kim's half sisters came and sat next to Kim's father!

By this time the expression "You could have blown me away with a feather" would have been a British understatement as Sarah and Danny's other kids came back and squeezed into the pew. *And by this time*, old Anna was sitting there just grinning.

I wasn't sure a sermon could say anything to me after what I saw, but I stood up with the others as the pastor came at his usual time and stood in his usual place at the front of the church and in what I assume was a usual start to the service, the Pastor announced the opening hymn, "All Glory, Laud and Honor."[3]

Anna took out her hanky that she had ironed for such an occasion, and oh she sang.

THE VISION

After church, I looked around, speechless. Danny and his recently wider family were having a great time talking about where they would go for dinner. Having had about all I could take of family at this point, I phoned by husband who was back in Florida and told him I was heading out to the dessert for a little thinking time before I got on the plane to head home. I wanted to walk and kick up some dust and have a little discussion of my own with Father God.

Ages ago, the Father had told me that one of the reasons He had chosen the Jewish people as His own was that they were real with Him. No messing about, they complained and they let Him have it! They shared the truth in their troubled minds. There was no cover up, no little sweetened-up chat about the state of their hearts. He was God, and the Jewish people knew that meant He was the truth, and He could take the truth from them. I still had much to learn about being real with God.

Walking around in a little patch of uncivilized Texas desert brought me to my senses. I could smell the dust. I cut off a weed or two and chewed on it. With sunglasses on and my hands in my pockets, I kicked dust like sand on a beach. God and I had spent beach time together, but here in the desert I could see He was bringing me back to Ezekiel once again.

"Why, just why am I so angry," I demanded of God. It should have been a lovely scene, complete with Hollywood music, to see this reunited family in church on a Sunday, and here I was mad as a Texas queen bee without any honey.

"Be a bone picker," I heard Him say.

"And that would be?" I said as grouchy as I felt, but I looked around for dead carcasses of cattle.

I walked as much anger out of me as I could, but all around me I saw the Ezekiel bones of my imagination. "Maybe I read too much!"

I began to shout, safe in the knowledge that there was no human for miles around. "Maybe I've dreamed some stupidly impossible dream of family restoration due to my own divorce and the hurt I have seen in my own children," I ranted. "And Father God, I know firsthand how the enemy has come to destroy family life in this generation as never before and did I think for one crazy second I could do something about it! Have I been arrogant in thinking all anyone had to do was declare God as God and some miracle would happen? Miraculously we would all live happily ever after? Sexual addiction would go away, drug addiction would be a thing of the past, everyone would be faithful and live with their commitments!" I was shocked to hear myself.

Shocked, but not stopping in my anger, "Why did I see what I saw on that church pew today? Why did You let me see this family come together? Do you *have any idea* what has to change in hearts and minds for anyone to even *want* to be in church together, not to mention talking about worshiping together?"

In a fleeting second I received a glimpse of the struggle—the sacrifice of pride and agendas and justice required to bring everyone to even to have a shared lunch here on earth, but the words, "Thy Kingdom come" and "Thou preparest a table" touched my heart and won out on the battlefield of my mind. He was calling me to this type of sacrifice.

"Go beyond the brokenness," I heard the Holy Spirit say in my spirit.

In my heart I knew I had already said "yes" to this ministry of family reconciliation on the day of my mother's funeral; but on this day, I had a small understanding of what a calling it would be. It would be hard to be in the same room with some people, and yet the Father would require more than tolerance. He wanted unconditional love and a shared meal.

I felt the hand of the Lord upon me, touching my eyes to see what He would see. I could see the ground around me was full of bones. Bones everywhere, littered among Coke cans. And He got hold of me and said, "Walk around them."

"I've read Ezekiel, Lord. I can in no way do this. I am not a prophet. I am just an ordinary follower of Jesus." I was deeply upset in my spirit.

"How could I dare gain from His reward?" The song came.

"I do not have an answer," the words and notes played havoc in my head.

He, the living Lord, my Brother Jesus, the Holy Spirit led me around, in and out of the driest of bones, and eventually I stopped kicking up the sand storm. I began to see the bones and remember the Scripture.

"Can these bones live?"

"O Sovereign Lord, only You know."

"Why don't you pick one up?" said my Shepherd.

I bent down and began to draw an imaginary bone in the dust. "I can't pick this up, Lord. I am not Ezekiel."

"Write on the bone," He said, and immediately He told me to write, "Everyone out, everyone back."

Instantly, I could picture the BBC commentator standing on an aircraft carrier in the Falklands. Unable to announce the number of British warplanes deployed in the battle, Brian Hannrahan found a clever way of letting the British people know on the evening news that all planes that went out that day had made it home. For me, I knew this meant that every child of mine, every family member who went out in the world was to come home to the Father. That was to be my focus and most important assignment in life. He had it written on a bone for me to pick.

"Would you like to pick another bone?" the Holy One asked. He had an outstretched, nail-scarred hand. In His mercy He said, "You can do this."

"If you think so, Lord. Another bone."

And the Word of the Lord came to me that for each bone He allowed me to pick, I was to take it slowly and lift the bone to the Father.

By the power of the Holy Spirit, I could prophesy His Word of life over the bones in my valley. I could look at the debris of shattered lives and pray His hope into each situation.

I knew from the Scriptures that I must declare Scripture over each bone, asking the Father to read me the name on each bone and asking Him how I should pray, praying to see His dream, praying to see way beyond broken dreams and see His dream for their lives.

"Say to this bone," I heard Him say deep in my spirit, "Dry bone, hear the Word of the Lord!"

Each child of mine had their name on a bone.

Each member of my family, near or extended, had a name on a bone. We were meant to be whole, connected to the body of Christ, not broken but whole.

I crumbled onto a bit of grass and didn't care about the dust. In my heart it was beyond me that the Father would have such a treasure for me; such peace in knowing in my life assignment of family reconciliation.

"I'm a bone picker," I said with the peace of one knowing my life assignment.

"But Lord, I don't know how to do this," I said, recognizing that picking up a bone from a dry valley and lifting it to the Lord for Him to breathe life into its marrow was sounding a little crazy. I got up from the ground, dusted myself off, and went back to the car. This bone picker had a plane to catch.

Danny met me at the airport. With security these days, there was no way we could do more than have a quick cup of coffee and say goodbye. But at least I could take a few minutes and ask him, "What happened?"

"Sarah made it easy," he said. "When she was away praying those couple of days, she remembered how her own mother had reached out to everyone. Anna never stood for much nonsense, and she always thought it was nonsense if your personal hurts stood in the way of someone coming to know the Lord and becoming part of a church family."

"I thought most Texas women would have run the *other woman* out of town!" I laughed. "But seriously, how does someone get that grace, that understanding that enables that kind of grace?"

"Sarah saw that grace while growing up. That grace, that mercy that only God could do, she realized she had seen all her life in Anna. Humanly speaking we can't get over ourselves enough to put the needs of others before our own needs. Yet, she had seen it time and time again demonstrated in Anna."

I thought back for a minute about how hard it was for me to feel racist because of what my parents had demonstrated by their lives. It had just never occurred to me to leave someone out of my life due to their skin color; yet as an adult, I had seen many people struggle with racism. But unfaithfulness? I had never seen Mom and Dad as much as have an argument over what was for dinner, never mind tough issues in marriage.

"As you can probably guess," Danny continued, "Anna was hardly a perfect parent; but she demonstrated loving everybody in her family. She never let someone's sexual sin or family bust-up keep her from loving you. If you are even remotely related, you are someone she is responsible before God to love and care for. Thankfully for me, she passed that down to Sarah."

"Our family was never like that," I said. "We'd cut you off as soon as look at you. Look at Julia and John. Who even knows where they go for Christmas."

"Not your Mom," snapped Danny.

"True," I agreed, and thought about the names on some of the bones the Lord had shown me.

"Sarah said that she hasn't always been this focused on how God wanted her to reach out to the lost. It was when she gave her life to Jesus that she became more concerned for the hurting and the lost than her own needs. She said she was more interested in introducing Kim to Jesus than worrying about some affair I had. She trusts God to meet every need. Man, I take my hat off to her."

"And she trusts you," I said, "some women couldn't do what I saw at church this morning. I imagine some women wouldn't want to be sitting with their husband's ex-wife."

"Ex-mistress," Danny corrected me.

"Whatever…"

Danny smiled, "She trusts God for giving her a sense of my heart. Believe me, she will give me a tap if she thinks I'm looking at another woman. She says she knows, has some discernment that God gave her as my helpmate, my wife."

Beyond Broken Families at Church

Back in our little town in Florida, I was challenged with asking God how I could get from my way of thinking to an understanding of *how* God wants me to be that demonstration of His love in my life. As part of my quiet time, which I dedicated to reading and praying and walking, trying to "get this understanding" from the Lord, I suddenly realized that I "happen" to attend what I now call "a bone picker church." The Holy Spirit had led me and my husband to be part of a church that is dedicated to reaching beyond the brokenness of family life in the world today to the healing of Jesus Christ.

With great clarity, I noticed that what was and is a warm and friendly church, was also a church that had opened its doors to some unusual people. I knew the church had great warmth and friendliness, but I suddenly had an awareness that this is a church where members greet ex-wives and sons-in-law at the door and nearly drag them in to a warm welcome.

This is where a grandmother drives for hours because a son said he would finally speak to her and then fresh out of prison would come live with her—and where the women's ministry shouts with joy because they have been praying for that kind of prison breakthrough for months, if not years. It is a church where men and women who have known what it is like to pace the floor with babies in the night, now do the night walk for baby Christians. They are bone pickers; people who have been in the valley and have come before the Lord saying

"Give me someone who wants to go to Your healing high pasture." Bone pickers are like Marines in that they are dedicated to "no buddy left behind." No one who runs away or hides or bolts is to be written off. No one is to be put into the too hard basket.[4]

"How do I learn to reach out to others, showing them this high healing pasture?" I asked the Father.

"Well…," He said, "remember what you learned about forgiveness?"

"Yes."

"And the Wall of Hostility?"

"Yes."

"And reconciliation?" He continued.

"Yes."

"And anger?"

"That too. I remember Lord."

Then I could "hear" Him smile. "Well, practice. With each bone you pick up and name and decree My word and pray over, you will use all you know; and I will teach you new things." He said in my heart.

I need to stay close to others who desire a life beyond the damage of brokenness—sharing encouragement for the tough days and knowledge for what I need to learn. We work best in a team. Not every church welcomes this kind of teamwork, but those that do have a deep love for recovery and reconciliation. In my spirit, I felt the Holy Spirit tell me, "They are a church after God's own heart."

I have learned that those who reach out to Christ, acknowledging His body, broken for us, make the church a house of prayer. They—we—have little time for programs or rituals, but all the time in the world for those who are hurting. They—we—lift up the lost before the Father. They—and by that I am learning would be me— care more for the hurting and the lost than their own feelings or their own pride and peace of mind. Together we are learning how to feed hungry people and carry those desiring to make it to the high pasture of healing. We have some good news to share.

There are some sacred keys to this Kingdom. The Father's love is for the healing of the nations; and when we (no more "they") say they have a bone to pick with you, it is for the joining of hands to lift the spirit of someone who was as good as dead and speak life of the Holy Spirit into his or her spirit, soul, and body.

And if the lost are so broken they can't find their way to the door of the faithful, we—the forgiven and reconciled to the Living Lord— are sent out to find them.

EPILOGUE

I would not leave you at this point, in a modern-day testimony of Ezekiel prophecy, simply standing in the desert, lifting up a bone of contention with shafts of prayer decreed over a loved one. The Father would not have you do this journey alone. If you are considering your own mission, which is humanly impossible but possible with Him, ask Him for help.

Ask Him who is to be your Aaron and your Hur, helping hold up your hands in prayer for a loved one—not taking over what the Father would have you pray, but strengthening your own praying hands.

Ask the Father to send you divine appointments set by His divine networking for counsel. Prayer ministry, trained listening and professional Christian counselors are all available to walk this journey with you. If in the natural sense, money is a block to what you believe you need, ask Father God to bring you what you need according to His dream with no expense spared. He is a generous Father who loves to give good gifts to His children, but no matter what comes your way, always ask, "Is this for me, Father?"

I was part of church leadership when my family fell apart, and it was some comfort that the pastor invited me to continue to take communion. To be fair, at that time neither of us knew what recovery should look like in the context of the Church of England. In our church, there was no trained prayer ministry or counseling team for family issues.

It is my hope that the church worldwide will train to deal with brokenness, as in every nation and in every denomination we face increasing challenges in the breakup of Christian family life. It is my hope that I and all who have received comfort and healing from the Shepherd, will have the courage to share the good news of the Father's high healing pasture.

May the Father put a new heart in all of us! (See Ezekiel 36:26.)

ENDNOTES

Chapter I: The Dream

1. Joachim Bar, *Meine Berufung: Gottes Traum für mein Leben* (Germany: Erf Verlag Gmbh & Company, 2011). Translation of title by Suzanne Hubers: "My Calling: God's Dream for My Life," in support of her husband, Ludgar Huber's sermon on God's Dream, used with kind permission of Ludgar, "Louie." This sermon, which inspired many including myself who heard it at Frensham Baptist Fellowship in 2011, inspired me to apply the principles to marriage.

2. Nicky and Sila Lee, *The Marriage Book* (London: Alpha International Publications, 2005), 16-17. For additional discussion on this subject, I recommend Dr. Douglas E. Rosenau's book, *A Celebration of Sex* (Nashville, TN: Thomas Nelson, 2002), starting at page x, in the Introduction. Dr. Rosenau states, "The loving, intimate relationship of you and your spouse is modeled after the relationship of God and His chosen people. ...Marriage is not a simple contract, but a deep vow and promise."

3. Roz Parker, from her sermon at Frensham Baptist Fellowship 2011, "Do Everything in Love—First Corinthians 16:14, Love Actually." Further discussion of Jesus' agape love is also found in Nancy Groom's book, *Married without Masks* (UK: Scripture Press Foundation Ltd., 1989), 58.

4. Ibid.

5. Lee, *The Marriage Book*, 23, which quotes from the excellent book, *Marriage as God Intended* by Selwyn Hughes (UK: Kingsway Publications 1983), 13. In Selwyn Hugh's 2005 edition, printed as part of "Life Journey," an Imprint of Cook Communication Ministries and Kingsway Communications Ltd, Hughs states on page 196 that, "it is important to understand that because marriage was laid down in creation, it has a permanent and not just temporary validity. In other words, it is God's order for His creation. Those who prefer to take the way of cohabitation rather than committing themselves to marriage violate that order and are under the condemnation of God."

CHAPTER 2: HOLY TRINITY BROMPTON, MONDAY NIGHT

1. Statistics on first, second, and third divorce rates from research units and governmental records around the world are found at www.divorcerate.org; accessed May 26, 2011.

2. For a discussion paper on the biblical job description of church leaders, read Bob Young's paper on Church Leadership at: http://www.bobyoungresources.com/leadership/church-leaders_what-do-they-do.pdf; accessed May 26, 2011. Also read Acts 20 and Ephesians 4.

3. In this case, bearing with one another in love (see Eph. 4:3), speaking the truth in love, (see Eph. 4:15) so that there is spiritual maturity.

4. See John 10:14.

5. For further reading on this topic, see Joachim Bar, *Meine Berufung: Gottes Traum für mein Leben* (Germany: Erf Verlag Gmbh & Company, 2011). Translation of title by Suzanne Hubers: "My Calling: God's Dream for My Life," and see Ezekiel 34:11-16.

6. Ezekiel 34:26 especially speaks of the Father's plans for blessings, "…I will send down showers of blessing," for

you are "wonderfully made" (Ps. 139:14). In Ezekiel 34, the Father says, "I Myself will search for My sheep and look after them;" but we are not to "trample" on the good news of this healing place or "muddy the waters" that He has for our healing (Ezekiel 34:18-19).

7. See Ephesians 2:10 "For we are God's workmanship, created in Christ Jesus to do good works, which God prepared in advance for us to do." In Galatians 5:1 it says, "It is for freedom that Christ has set us free. Stand firm, then, and do not let yourselves be burdened again by a yoke of slavery."

CHAPTER 3: WHAT IT TAKES TO BE HEALED

1. "But the Comforter, which is the Holy Ghost, whom the Father will send in My name, He shall teach you all things, and bring all things to your remembrance, whatsoever I have said unto you" (John 14:26 KJV). In the NIV, the word "Comforter" is translated as "Counselor," but in verse 27 it goes on to say that this Counselor brings peace, "Peace I leave with you; My peace I give you. I do not give to you as the world gives. Do not let your hearts be troubled and do not be afraid."

2. Psalm 27:10 says, "Though my father and mother forsake me, the Lord will receive me." Verse 11 continues with that even though someone is "forsaken" by parents, we may call on the Lord to "Teach me Your way, O Lord...."

3. Visit www.htb.org.uk; accessed May 26, 2011

4. "Parents on the Move!" by Kathleen McAnear Smith, Destiny Image Europe Publishing.

5. This song was originally published in 1834 in "The Spirit of the Psalms," and is a paraphrase of Psalm 103. Now in the public domain, the first verse reads:

Praise my soul, the King of heaven;
To His feet they tribute bring.

Ransomed, healed, restored, forgiven,
Evermore His praises sing: Alleluia! Alleluia! Praise the
everlasting King.

CHAPTER 4: LET THE SABBATICAL BEGIN!

1. Ellel Pierrepont is the Frensham, Surrey campus of Ellel
   Ministries UK and is a registered charity (Scottish Charity Commission), The Christian Trust. Ellel Ministries
   UK was founded in 1986, led by Peter Horrobin, International Director of Ellel Ministries. In their vision they
   state, "Ellel Ministries is a non-denominational Christian mission organisation with a vision to resource and
   equip the Church by welcoming people, teaching them
   about the Kingdom of God and healing those in need."
   Visit www.ellelministries.org; accessed May 26, 2011.

2. Visit www.NeverEverTheSame.com; accessed May 26,
   2011. This Luke Nine Eleven Training School is a one-
   year residential program run in four ten-week stages at
   Ellel Pierrepont.

3. Luke 10:38-42 says, "As Jesus and His disciples were on
   their way, He came to a village where a woman named
   Martha opened her home to Him. She had a sister called
   Mary, who sat at the Lord's feet listening to what He
   said. But Martha as distracted by all the preparations
   that had to be made. She came to Him and asked, 'Lord,
   don't You care that my sister has left me to do the work
   by myself? Tell her to help me!' 'Martha, Martha,' the
   Lord answered, 'You are worried and upset about many
   things, but only one thing is needed. Mary has chosen
   what is better, and it will not be taken away from her.'"

4. The Christian concept of "equal yoking" comes from
   Second Corinthians 6:14-18 which reads, "Do not be
   yoked together with unbelievers. For what do righteousness and wickedness have in common? Or what fellowship can light have with darkness? What harmony is
   there between Christ and Belial? What does a believer

have in common with an unbeliever? What agreement is there between the temple of God and idols? For we are the temple of the living God. As God has said, 'I will live with them and walk among them, and I will be their God, and they will be My people.'"

5. I have often heard Peter Horrobin refer to his vision of Ellel as a "teaching hospital for the emotionally wounded."

6. This refers to John 4 and the story of the Samaritan woman meeting Jesus at the well, when in John 4:15 the woman says, "Sir, give me this water so that I won't get thirsty and have to keep coming here to draw water." Jesus has told her, in verse 14, "but whoever drinks the water I give him will never thirst. Indeed, the water I give him will become in him a spring of water welling up to eternal life."

7. These notes were part of those given during the NETS course (The Luke Nine Eleven Training School). Visit www.NeverEverTheSame.com. Further information on this topic may also be found as part of the online course provided by Ellel Ministries UK, www.ellelministries.org/365; accessed June 18, 2011.

8. In other words, I could go from having a godly boldness as demonstrated by Elijah in First Kings 18 where Elijah had complete confidence in the Lord when he said on Mount Carmel in verse 24, "Then you call on the name of your god, and I will call on the name of the Lord. The god who answers by fire—he is God"; and then Elijah in the very next chapter became afraid and ran! In First Kings 19:3-4 it says, "Elijah was afraid and ran for his life. When he came to Beersheba in Judah, he left his servant there, while he himself went a day's journey into the desert. He came to a broom tree, sat down under it and prayed that he might die. 'I have had enough Lord,' he said. 'Take my life; I am no better than my ancestors.'"

9. This is in reference to Revelation 3:21 when Jesus says, "To him who overcomes, I will give the right to sit with

Me on My throne, just as I overcame and sat down with My Father on His throne."

CHAPTER 5: FORGIVENESS

1. Though this story is in the public domain, by virtue of the fact that I first heard this story on the evening news, and this version of the story is my own rendition, there are other versions that may be of interest to some, and so I include here a reference to the *London Times* article, "What I've learnt about husbands," July 9, 2006; http://www.timesonline.co.uk/tol/news/article684946.ece; accessed May 26, 2011.

2. This is in reference to Ellel Ministries Pierrepont; www.ellelministries.org.

3. My original recovery course was with Holy Trinity Brompton, and was entitled, "Divorce and Separation Recovery," of which more information may be found on the Holy Trinity Brompton Website: www.htb.org.uk.

4. For more information on the vision of Peter Horrobin and Ellel Ministries please visit www.ellelministries.org.

5. In Ephesians 6:12 it says, "For our struggle is not against flesh and blood, but against the rulers, against the authorities, against the powers of this dark world and against the spiritual forces of evil in the heavenly realms."

6. www.ellelministries.org

7. According to Strong's Online Concordance, the word "agape" means affection or benevolence, specially a love feast.

8. Gary Chapman, *Five Languages of Apology* (Chicago: Northfield Publishing, 2006).

9. Ibid.

10. In Luke 5:20 says, "When Jesus saw their faith He said, 'Friend, your sins are forgiven'"; but with those who crucified Him, He prayed in Luke 23:34 that the Father would

forgive them in the future, stating, "Father forgive them, for they do not know what they are doing." With the robber expressing faith next to Jesus on the cross, in contrast to Jesus' stance on forgiveness with the soldiers, He said, "Today you will be with Me in paradise" (Luke 23:43).

11. Ephesians 4:26, "In your anger do not sin: Do not let the sun go down while you are still angry."

Chapter 6: The Wall of Hostility

1. Visit www.htb.org.uk.

2. Ezekiel 34:12, "As a shepherd looks after his scattered flock when he is with them, so will I look after My sheep. I will rescue them from all the places where there scattered on a day of clouds and darkness."

3. Ellel Ministries UK Centres; www.ellelministries.org.

4. See Ephesians 2:14 (NKJV).

Chapter 7: The High Pasture

1. From 1969 to 1974, "The Brady Bunch" was a television program about the misadventures of two families blended into one family. Both parents had been widowed and married again. I always thought this large, fantasy family gave apt demonstration that a housekeeper was needed!

2. Acts 16:31 says, "They replied, 'Believe in the Lord Jesus, and you will be saved—you and your household.'" This chapter of Acts continues in verse 34 with, "The jailer brought them into his house and set a meal before them; he was filled with joy because he had come to believe in God—he and his whole family." All the family, as noted in verse 33, were baptized.

3. John 10:27 says, "My sheep listen to My voice; I know them, and they follow Me."

4. In John 16:33 Jesus says, "I have told you these things, so that in Me you may have peace. In this world you will

have trouble. But take heart! I have overcome the world." This concept of overcoming is from Jesus, who shows us that when He says He is "the way and the truth and the life" in John 14:6. Jesus tells us that as we follow Him, we have hope of becoming "overcomers." "To him who overcomes, I will give the right to sit with Me on My throne, just as I overcame and sat down with My Father on His throne" (Rev. 3:21).

5. John Bevere's book, *Thus Sayeth the Lord?* says, "Have we become like the prophets in the days of Jeremiah and Ezekiel, who prophesied peace and prosperity, while God endeavoured to call His people back to His heart?" (Point 23 in Kindle book publication by Charisma House, Strang Company, Lake Mary, FL).

6. Ezekiel 34:14, "I will tend them in a good pasture...."

7. In Ezekiel 34:15 it says, "I Myself will tend My sheep and have them lie down, declares the Sovereign Lord." This is a safe place in that we can rest, due to His care.

8. I refer to the 2009 film *The Blind Side*, directed by John Lee Hancock, starring Sandra Bullock, Tim McGraw, and Quinton Aaron.

9. Ezekiel 34:14 states, "...they will feed in a rich pasture on the mountains of Israel."

10. In the King James Version, a good pasture is a "fat pasture," noting, "They found fat pasture and good," in First Chronicles 4:40. And in Ezekiel 34:14 (KJV), "I will feed them in a good pasture, and upon the high mountains of Israel shall their fold be: there shall they lie in a good fold, and in a fat pasture shall they feed upon the mountains of Israel."

11. In no way do I intend to cast dispersions on good, professional counseling; in fact, should you consider taking on a ministry to your own family, I highly recommend professional Christian counseling. To give clarity to what I am suggesting, I want to state that we need to listen to the

Holy Spirit's guidance in this matter and not just follow a popular culture. In Isaiah 50:11 it talks about people who "light [their own] fires," and "provide yourselves with flaming torches," not as those in Isaiah 51:1 who "pursue righteousness and who seek the Lord." We need the Father's guidance, according to His Word, when we seek counsel.

12. John Bevere's book, *Thus Sayeth the Lord?* says, "Have we become like the prophets in the days of Jeremiah and Ezekiel, who prophesied peace and prosperity, while God endeavored to call His people back to His heart?" (Point 23 in kindle book publication by Charisma House, Strang Company, Lake Mary, FL.)

13. I am not aware of when I first heard the expression, "knowing in your knower," but I clearly remember Jill Southern Jones using this term when referring to knowing something deep down inside your spirit whether something is right or wrong. Jill is director of Ellel Pierrepont, of Ellel Ministries UK. Visit www.ellelminitries.org.

14. From Hillsong Australia's, Mighty to Save; http://www.keepandshare.com/htm/music_lyrics/christian/mighty_to_save.php; accessed May 26, 2011.

15. I have heard Joyce Meyer talk about "going around the mountain one more time," so many times on her television show that I hardly know where to source the quote, so I will simply provide her Website: http://www.joycemeyer.org/ and urge you to listen and learn! She bases this Scripture on Deuteronomy 2:3 where it says, "You have made your way around this hill country long enough..." Joyce Meyer, *New Day, New You: 366 Devotions for Enjoying Everyday Life* (Faithworks, 2007).

16. Deuteronomy 34:1 is a good place to start. See also Psalm 18:2.

17. Dr. Martin Luther King Jr., "Mountain Top" speech on YouTube.   http://www.youtube.com/watch?v=wzG3 VMTGRVA; accessed May 26, 2011.

18. Though the word "ravine" is used in Ezekiel 34:13b ("I will pasture them on the mountains of Israel, in the ravines, and in all the settlements in the land."), it was used more recently in modern times in 1772, first appearing as a French word meaning "a small narrow steep-sided valley that is larger than a gully and smaller than a canyon and that is usually worn by running water";   http://www.merriam-webster.com/dictionary/ravines; accessed May 26, 2011. *The Oxford Pocket Dictionary,* p. 747, calls a ravine a "deep narrow gorge." For further reading, please note "Guide to Protecting Urban Ravines" compiled by A Community for Ravine Areas, 2004; Friends of Ravines, contributors to the Guide include Nancy S. McAleer, BS, Landscape Horticulture and Mayhew Scholar at the Ohio State University. I discussed this exciting topic with Richard Martin of the Nature Conservancy, www.tnc.org, who explained that, "Whenever we are looking at restoration in nature, we have to be concerned about the effects on human communities," and that Louisiana has the largest flood plain (larger area than a ravine) restoration project in the States. Increasingly, conservationists are aware of the need of these physical restoration areas.

19. Ibid.

20. http://www.eoearth.org/article/Riparian_zone; accessed May 23, 2011.

21. Amanda Wildgoose, Glenn Waller, Sue Clarke, Alex Reid, "Psychiatric Symptomatology in Borderline and Other Personality Disorders," *Journal of Nervous & Mental Disease:* November 2000, Volume 188, Issue 11, pp 757-763; http://journals.lww.com/jonmd/Fulltext/2000/11000/Psychiatric_Symptomatology_in_Borderline_and_Other.6.aspx; accessed May 26, 2011.

For a Christian perspective on this disorder, visit: http://www.associatedcontent.com/article/131104/multiple_personality_disorder_a_christian.html?cat=72; accessed May 26, 2011. Please remember this is a psychiatric disorder and we can use these terms without knowing what we truly mean. Terms such as "disassociation" and "fragmentation" need professional psychiatric diagnosis. I simply use the term "fragmented" in this paragraph to bring this issue into the conversation when searching for causes of family breakdown. Please remember that Christ is our hope, even for those who in the natural sense seem beyond hope.

22. www.NeverEverTheSame.com.

Chapter 8: Listening and Boundaries

1. While there are many Websites that give you parts of this famous speech, it is very much worth taking a moment to read Dr. King's "Dream Speech" in entirety; http://www.americanrhetoric.com/speeches/mlkihavedream.htm; accessed May 26, 2011.

2. The classic boundary book would be on anyone's recommended reading list, *Boundaries: When to Say Yes, How to Say No to Take Control of Your Life* by Dr. Henry Cloud and Dr. John Townsend (Grand Rapids, MI: Zondervan, 1992).

3. Nehemiah, chapter 3.

4. University of Pennsylvania, African Studies Center, copy of 1963 Letter From Birmingham Jail by Dr. Martin Luther King Jr. http://www.africa.upenn.edu/Articles_Gen/Letter_Birmingham.html

5. Ibid., paragraph six.

6, Ibid., paragraph seven.

7. Ibid., paragraph seven.

8. Ibid., paragraph nine.

9. Colossians 1:20, "and through Him to reconcile to Himself all things, whether things on earth or things in heaven, by making peace through His blood, shed on the cross." And Ephesians 2:14, "For He Himself is our peace, who has made the two one and has destroyed the barrier, the dividing wall of hostility."

10. Dr. Russ Parker, sermon on "Boundaries," Frensham Baptist Fellowship, Frensham, Surrey, United Kingdom, 2010.

CHAPTER 9: WHY?

1. This story used by kind permission of Dr. Russ Parker, Director of Acorn Christian Healing Foundation, which has partnerships in twelve nations, the newest in the United States called Christian Listeners USA:

A woman called Joy who was a member of the Burundian government was thrown into jail during the long civil war. There she was systematically tortured, beaten, and raped. Her family largely perished although some managed to escape from the country. When she was eventually released, she went to see her Catholic priest who told her that she must forgive her enemies who abused her so badly. Joy, however, said that the priest was not really interested in her forgiving her enemies. He just did not want to listen to her pain. Consequently, Joy lost her faith and was nearing despair. Then one day she attended an Acorn listening conference in Bujumbura where she sat down with the tutor of that day, a lady called Joanna. All the time Joy poured out her story she expected to be interrupted with advice or prayers, but this did not happen. Joanna simply listened. It was during this time of sharing that Joy noticed a man sitting at the back of the room who gradually came farther forward as she told Joanna her tale. He got so close that Joy asked Joanna, "Who is the friend you brought with you?" Joanna turned around and saw no one. Joy had seen Jesus. It was that moment of recognition when she suddenly realized what Jesus was doing on the cross, He was listening to the pain of the whole world, past, present, and future, and her own. It was an incredible healing for her to realize that Jesus hadn't come to tell her how bad she was but to listen to her story because she was worth listening to. It healed her wounded heart and transformed her life. She is now a Listening teacher herself and was greatly used by God to help end the 13-year civil war when she helped mediate the cease fire through teaching the various civil war generals how to listen to one another.

2. This story was given in a talk by Reverend Charles Rowley on a Celebrate Recovery evening at First Christian Church, Venice, Florida, in 2010. Used by kind permission.

3. My husband and I belong to two churches, one in Florida and one in England. It is the Florida church, Fisherman's Net Revival Center, led by Doctors Jim and Joy McInnis that is mentioned here.

4. The Message version of the Bible.

5. For further discussion on the Greek and Hebrew definitions of the word "hear" in the Bible, please note CARM: Christian Apologetics and Research ministry: http://carm.org/paul-hear-voice; accessed May 26, 2011.

6. In addition to Ezekiel 34, Psalm 107:13-14 says, "Then they cried to the Lord in their trouble. And He saved them from their distress. He brought them out of darkness and the deepest gloom and broke away their chains."

7. The American Academy of Childhood and Adolescent Psychiatry Website: http://www.aacap.org/ has a range of research on this subject. I also recommend reading Helena Wilkinson's book, *Beyond Chaotic Eating* (MarshallPickering Publishing, first published in Great Britain 1993). Helena Wilkinson is a member of the British

Association of Counselling and the Association of Christian Counsellors.

8. Leviticus 23:4: "These are the Lord's appointed feasts, the sacred assemblies you are to proclaim at their appointed times." In the New Testament, in Luke 14:12-24, Jesus talks about inviting people to a wedding feast. In First Corinthians 11:24 (KJV), Jesus speaks the words, "This is My body, which is broken for you."

9. First Corinthians 9:27: "No, I beat my body and make it my slave so that after I have preached to others. I myself will not be disqualified for the prize."

CHAPTER 10: THY KINGDOM COME

1. I am not kidding.

2. These talks were based on Dr. Myles Munroe's book, *Kingdom Principles: Preparing for Kingdom Experience and Expansion*; Understanding the Kingdom (Shippensburg, PA: Destiny Image Publishers, 2007).

3. Ibid.

4. Ibid., 161.

5. Ibid., 160.

6. Mrs. Linda LeSourd Lader is pastor of Second Presbyterian Church in Fort Lauderdale, Florida. From 1993 to 1996, she assisted with White House liaison to American communities of faith and advised the U.S. President on public policy issues pertaining to religion. Mrs. Lader's education includes Yale Divinity School where she was a Fellow at the Yale Center for Faith and Culture. Her editing work continues the tradition of her parents— Leonard LeSourd, founding editor of *Guideposts* and Catherine Marshall, author of *A Man Called Peter, Christy,* and other best-selling books. From: http://www.renaissanceweekend.org/site/aboutus/founders.htm; accessed June 18, 2011.

7. Linda LeSourd Lader very kindly gave me permission to use this story.

CHAPTER 11: FREQUENT FLYER

1. Opening lines from the film, "Love Actually," by Richard Curtis, St. Martin's Griffin, 2003 http://www.aacap.org/page.ww?section=system&name=Search+Results&indexId=default&hitsStart=1&query=food+addictions&x=7&y=7; accessed May 24, 2011.

2. For the history of the modern hospice movement, visit: http://www.rowanshospice.co.uk/index.php?id=13; accessed May 26, 2011.

3. For more information about Village on the Isle, and to read their mission statement, visit: http://www.villageontheisle.com/; accessed May 26, 2011.

4. The term "accountability partner," is used in this chapter as meaning someone with whom I prayed and gave permission to assist me in reaching my own goal of living according to God's Holy Word.

5. See First Peter 2:12.

6. See Proverbs 4:22 and Proverbs 19:8.

7. See Second Corinthians 6:14.

8. In Matthew 19:6 it says, "So they are no longer two but one. Therefore what God has joined together, let man not separate." In Mark 10:9 it also says, "Therefore what God has joined together, let man not separate." We are to respect what God has joined together, nothing in our words or deeds should separate that bond.

9 In Matthew 24:43 it talks about guarding your house from the thief. Some of us need to more than shut the door on the enemy who would rob our families (see John 10:10 for satan's job description), we need to lock that door!

10. This is a reference to Ezekiel 34:20, where there are "fat sheep" who have received healing in the Father's healing

place and have plenty to share, but do not share the good news of the Father's healing.

11. See Psalm 61:4 and Psalm 91:1-2.

12. Visit www.joycemeyerministries.com.

13. Psalm 116:15, "Precious in the sight of the Lord is the death of His saints."

14. See John 14:2-3.

15. From the *Church of England Prayer Book.*

CHAPTER 12: THE BONE PICKER

1. Luke Nine Eleven Training School is a one-year residential program run in four ten-week stages at Ellel Pierrepont.

2. A childhood story about a cobbler who made shoes for all the children in his village except for his own.

3. "The original hymn was written by Theodulph of Orleans in A.D. 820-821. Theodulph was a bishop in the ninth century who was imprisoned, wrongly accused of conspiracy against the King," according to British history of hymns. He is reported to have written this hymn while in prison. The translation into more modern English was in 1851 by John M. Neale. Source: http://www.know-britain.com/hymns/all_glory_laud_honour.htm; accessed May 26, 2011.

4. Jill Southern Jones of Ellel Pierrepont (www.ellelministries.org) has often expressed a desire to see that churches do not place anyone in what she calls a "too hard basket." By this term, she is referring to the fact that "nothing is too hard for God!" Quoted with kind permission of Jill Southern Jones, 2011.

ABOUT THE AUTHOR

For over 30 years, Kathleen McAnear Smith has lived and worked as a teacher overseas. She was born and raised in Washington, DC and continued her education at Stetson University in Florida, the School of International Service at American University, and a winter term at the University of Moscow. Kathleen also served as a Peace Corps Volunteer and high school teacher in Jamaica.

Since 1976, Kathleen relocated to five areas of the United Kingdom, experiencing re-entry to the United States and then returned to England, where she raised her daughter and son. During this time, she achieved an MSc in Social Policy at the University of Southampton, taught school, and created her own successful consulting business, Childtrack UK Ltd., which became internationally recognized by the CNN Business Traveller program in 2004. Childtrack specialized in relocating families primarily in the financial sectors of London and New York, with families coming in from all over the world.

As a follower of Jesus Christ, Kathleen has a heart for global family life, based on being raised in a missionary family, and believes that mature and wiser women have a vital role to play in assisting today's corporate women and men in the international arena.

ANOTHER EXCITING TITLE OF
Kathleen McAnear Smith

PARENTS ON THE MOVE!
Preparing Your Family for a Successful and Creative Relocation

by Kathleen McAnear Smith

Parents on the Move! is filled with personal experiences, practical advice, specific information about schools, research trips, and much more to help every family make a successful move. The author shares insider information (and humorous stories) from her years of experience as successful relocation education consultant for families of all faiths.

ISBN: 978-88-89127-96-4

Additional copies of this book and other book titles
from DESTINY IMAGE™ EUROPE
are available at your local bookstore.

We are adding new titles every month!

To view our complete catalog online, visit us at:

www.eurodestinyimage.com

Send a request for a catalog to:

Via della Scafa 29/14
65013 Città Sant'Angelo (Pe) - ITALY
Tel. +39 085 4716623 ♦ +39 085 8670146
Fax: +39 085 9090113
info@eurodestinyimage.com

"Changing the world, one book at a time."™

Are you an author?
Do you have a "today" God-given message?

CONTACT US

We will be happy to review your manuscript
for the possibility of publication:

publisher@eurodestinyimage.com
http://www.eurodestinyimage.com/pages/AuthorsAppForm.htm